T0063115

Why I Am a
CHRISTIAN

REV. HENRY HARLIN, JR.

WESTBOW®
PRESS
A DIVISION OF THOMAS NELSON
& ZONDERVAN

WestBow Press books may be ordered through booksellers or by contacting:
WestBow Press
A Division of Thomas Nelson & Zondervan
1663 Liberty Drive
Bloomington, IN 47403
www.westbowpress.com
1 (866) 928-1240

ISBN: 978-1-4908-4668-2 (sc)
Library of Congress Control Number: 2014913647

Printed in the United States of America.

WestBow Press rev. date: 09/09/2014

Contents

Dedication

THIS BOOK IS DEDICATED TO MY MOTHER, THE LATE MRS. ROSIE LRENE HARLIN AND HER MOTHER, MY GRAND MOTHER, THE LATE MRS. ANNIE BRANDON, BOTH WHO ARE GREATLY RESPONSIBLE FOR MY SALVATION BECAUSE OF THEIR PRAYERS.

Forward

The Christian lives his/her life in the Spirit of faith. The things and events of their living is not according to what is in their sphere of known occurrence, in other words the Christian lives their life expecting God to work super natural works of His Spirit in their life.

Yet, the expectations of their faith are produced by the Holy Spirit as fruits of the Spirit in the Christians life and are predictable because the word of God in Scripture informs the believer to know what God wants them to know.

This is the faith on which the Christian stands and this faith has a foundation that is historical in the word that has been spoken and revealed under the oracles of The Living God.

The true and living God has given promises and enlightenment to inform His disciples and saints, that are guaranteed because the results and out comes of the promises are in the power and are demonstrated in the Being of God Himself.

There was nobody else of which God could guarantee the authority of His word, therefore He presented and established it's authority in Himself.

Hebrews Chapter 6: Verses 13 –20, (King James) "For when God made promise to Abraham, because He could swear by no greater, He swore by Himself, 14. Saying, Surely blessing I will bless thee, and multiplying I will multiply thee. 15. And, so, after he had patiently endured, he obtained the promise. 16. For men verily swear by the greater: and an oath for confirmation is to them an end of all strife. 17. Wherein God, willing more abundantly to show unto the heirs of promise the immutability of His counsel, confirmed it by an oath: 18. that by two immutable things, in which it was impossible for God to lie, we might have a strong consolation, who have fled for refuge to lay hold upon the hope set before us: 19. Which hope we have as an anchor of the soul, both sure and steadfast, and which entereth into that within the veil; 20. Whither the forerunner is for us entered, even Jesus, made a high Priest for ever after the order of Melchizedek."

So you see the Christian believer, he/she does not walk in a "leap of blind faith."

There are blessings in life promised by God through Jesus, and when in according to God's direction the Christian believes and anticipates, his/her life is under the supervision of God, they will receive victory according to the word of God.

The life of faith the Christian lives is summed up in Hebrews Chapter 11: verses 1-3, Now faith is the substance of things hoped for, the evidence of things not seen. 2. For by it the elders obtained a good report. 3. Through faith we understand that the worlds were framed by the word of God, so that things which are seen were not made of things which do appear. "Hebrews chapter 11: verses 1-3; King James Version

What I am saying is the Christian salvation is it's self embodied in God's willingness to grant by His own power salvation freely to the believer. God's gift of salvation is founded in the life of His Son: Jesus, and is given to the believer who trusts Jesus for salvation. Which is God's grace.

As the believer in Jesus studies the Scriptures as they mature in the Spiritual life of becoming more like Christ, more knowledge is gained, informing the Christian about who Jesus is. The Christian gains knowledge about Jesus' power and about Jesus' majesty and how Jesus is adequate to provide for the Christian salvation and preservation.

The believers trust is established with more revelation (light, Spiritual information) revealed in the word of God. The Apostle Paul exhorts us "to diligently study the word "that we might have a true comprehension of what we believe in our Christian doctrines.

The purpose of studying scripture is (1) to inform the believer of true and correct doctrine; (2) to equip the believer with doctrine in order to persevere in the living of every day life now; (3) to enable the Christian to have Christ's truths and His word to tell to other peoples: (4) to sustain the trust and staying power in the Christian in times of stress in life and most of all to adequately worship and praise God.

Why does the Christian only worship this one God? The answer is in the Scriptures.

What is accomplished by tithing? The answer is in the word.

What are the weapons of warfare for the believer and how do we use them? We study the Scriptures to discover the answers for these questions and so much more.

Of course there is so much more that anchors the believer' faith that is found in the word of God. We gain a fuller comprehension of what Christ means when He says He has all power. God expresses for us spiritual knowledge of His kingdom in order that the leap of faith for the Christian is not a blind leap.

God's word explains how the mind of God is not like our minds, for His mind is so much greater than our human mind.

Chapter 1

Introduction to Christianity: My Family Taught Some Things About Living for Christ: And there were Influences from other People: Also the Holy Spirit brought me into a Relationship with Jesus

Foremost and predominantly the reality of Christianity in my life is the work of the plan of God. Galatians 3: 1-14.

The process of growing into a Christian for many of us is a different set of events and circumstances. Each person is introduced to Christ in his or her own unique manner. Each experience is different.

On the human side of the circumstances; I was born into a lot of families who were practicing Christians. My earliest memories of worship was in a Holiest Assembly. The Pastor was a woman, worship was held in a tent in the back yard of the Pastor's property. People used tambourines to beat out the rhythm of the music. When many of the women got "caught up in The Spirit" they fell out on the ground that was covered with sawdust. Other women covered them with sheets on the ground. Meetings were

1

Sundays during the daylight hours: we broke for lunch. Each family contributed a dish for the church membership to eat. Later on in the afternoon we went back to worship, and the worship continued late into the night. There was singing, testifying, and the Pastor preached or another person preached. I can not recall if my biological mother attended this church. My mother died when I was six. After my mother died I lived with her mother, Mrs. Annie Brandon. My mother's name was Rosie Lrene Harlin.

During the time I lived with My grandmother I remember watching my grandmother pray on her knees and she was crying out to God. My grand mother did not drink or smoke. She taught me about Jesus and God and as much as she could and how to live a moral life. Of course, being a woman she had a challenge on her hands, because I was curious about the way people were living around me in the neighborhood and I wanted to discover things for my self. And many times I went against her advice. Again I would come home to find her on her knees praying.

She also believed in the power of the switch until I was too big to whip. She also rearranged her life to keep people out of our home who might be a wrong influence in my life. Once when I came home with a bag of candy, she asked me where did I get it from? I told her I had run a task for one of her neighbors; she went to the lady's house and asked her if that was what had happened, of course the answer was no. My grandmother finally learned that I had stole the candy from a local store; she made me return the candy back to the store owner and confess to sealing it.

A few years later, she joined a Seventh-Day Adventist Church. We learned the doctrines of the church: From sundown Friday night until sundown Saturday night was the Sabbath. She prepared the meals for Saturday on Friday; because we did not work or shop on Saturday. The meats we ate were chicken, fish, beef, liver, we did not eat catfish because it did not have scales; we ate a veggie meat made from soy products for health reasons.

We believed Christ died and arose for our salvation; we were baptized by emerging in the water and we celebrated The Lord's Supper. We believed in the Trinity and expected the return of Christ for His Church. We attended Camp meeting on the campus of Oak Wood College in Huntsville, Al.

I went with her to Missionary meetings and heard the songs sung in these meetings, most of them were the long standing hymns of the church. She also enrolled me in their Christian school, where Biblical teaching was a daily instruction. And we attended Sabbath School and worship service. I was able to participate in many programs in the church. One of which I remember singing with a couple other boys "We Three Kings."

During this time I was baptized at the age of ten.

It was while attending this church, one Sabbath afternoon, the Pastor mentioned to me; he had received a revelation that I would preach for Christ one day. I was around 9 years old, I really did not take his statement seriously at that time, because I did not have a working concept of what preaching meant. But it did make me recall that about a year earlier when I was playing in my living room I heard a distinct voice in my spirit from God telling me I would preach for The Lord one day, again I did not dwell on what I had heard.

I was more absorbed with the events occurring in school, like trying to keep up with my studies, of course fighting with kids on the way to school, while I at school, and on the way back home. There were bullies, our way of dealing with them was to stand up to them, we may not have won every battle, but as long as we fought back, they learned we were not afraid of them and we would not run away. And believe it or not the bully soon left us alone. I never told my grandmother about these fights. I don't know if she knew about them or not.

I can recall seeing the lunches that children brought from home and I wished I could have a lunch like that. I wanted to play in the band at school, but was told that my grades were not adequate, nor would I have the money to get an instrument to play.

I had a friend, Ross who was in high school, and ran track. I wanted to run track, but for the same reason of grades I was told I would have to improve my grade average. In spite of that Ross taught me about the techniques of running, how to train and develop my breathing and mental toughness while competing. That one activity helped instill esteem in me, because it gave me something I could do that I felt good in doing. In spite of the fact that my grandmother and I were poor, running made me fill I belonged. It is an activity I still participate in.

Growing up in the projects was a challenge. At that time in the 60's, many of the kids were joining gangs, each project had it's gang. If you were caught in another project the gang in that area would beat you up. I know it was the grace of God that I survived those days, because I traveled all over the city. Also in the 60's we were dealing with segregation.

Sit ins and demonstration were being held, even though in Huntsville thing were not as hectic as in other parts of the country, we had our difficulties. There was the threat of injury and death. Growing up in that type of conflict was one were the future was unstable and uncertain. There seemed to be a disconnect between what I was learning about Jesus and the things occurring in my life every day. I saw on t.v. and heard on the news how people were being treated and killed throughout the country and wondered if it would be safer to pick a way of violence in order to survive or how could the life of living for Christ protect us. These decisions were heavy on a young child to make on his own.

We had to deal with having food, and every day provisions with nobody in the family working.

Around the age of 12 I moved to live with my father's sister, Mrs. Alice love. Aunt Alice, her mother, Ida, my grandmother on my father's side, and aunt Alice's husband uncle Walter Love. They did not have any children and I was the only child in the household. My father had been the baby boy of aunt Alice's family and because of that she thought about me as she was doing something special for her brother, and of course she spoiled me.

Uncle Walter was an United Methodist Pastor, he pastured several rural churches. From time to time I attended these churches with him. While visiting in these churches I learned the order of worship was not as the other services in the other churches, although the order was not that different. I enjoyed the order of their worship. One thing was constant in every denomination's worship experience, it is "CHRIST IS THE FOCUS- AND THE AUTHOR OF SALVATION."

Basically my early years of life introduced me to the teachings of Christ; God and the Scriptures of the Bible. One thing I discovered while living with uncle Walter was something about being a Pastor. He was a compassionate man and in any way he could help anybody when he was asked, he would help. Lots of times I became angry with him because I felt people were taking advantage of him but he had a passion to help people.

Many times in the middle of the night I was awaken when he had received a call to go help some one; perhaps their house had burned down and he brought the family back to stay with us until they could find some place to move to.

I also learned while living with Uncle Walter, that the work for a Pastor has nothing to do with making a big salary. One thing I like about the Methodist Church is that the Pastor is guaranteed a salary. Yet, the salary depends on what the congregation is able to afford according to it's finances. This means a faithful Pastor must be motivated by something other than money.

I lived with Uncle Oscar and Aunt Nettie for a while.

Of course all of the Christian instruction came along with the social interaction of the world. The things that happened in every day life left a lot of questions concerning the Christian instructions I had learned. But what did develop was a real faith in God and in Jesus as protector and as a provider for my life as well as for my grandmother. My grandmother suffered with muscular sclerosis, I witness her health deteriorate from a healthy body to being paralyzed from her waist down. She was confined to her bed and a wheel chair. Most of her care had to be done for her by some one else. She received about $22.00 a month from my father's social security. we lived in the projects. I attended a public school early on in life, and those conditions served to develop a child's dependence of faith on God. Later on in life I discovered Christ had really preserved our life during my early years.

At the age of 18 I joined the Marine Corps and during boot camp the strength needed to graduate was provided by Christ. For the 1st. 2 weeks I was in shock but soon I realized that they were not going to kill me. The training was rigorous and physical as well as it had a mental bearing on me. My early faith training enabled me to have confidence that I could complete the basic training and in which I did.

During the 4 years of duty I ended up in Viet Nam. I was an Infantry man or what we called a ground ponder, during the year in Viet Nam my job was to walk the missions as the point man, which is any time my squad, platoon, and sometimes company had the lead I was the first man to lead out.

On my first day in the field, I was chosen to walk point. It was a company size operation, my platoon had point, we were to walk in the middle of a dried up river bed. My experience in watching movies was that walking behind trees provided cover, so I headed for the trees, I was told to go back to the river bed, after a while I headed back to the trees. At that time I was pulled off point and another Marine took point. He walked into a machine gun ambush, his head was shot off and the guy behind him guts were shot out. The ambush was aimed down the dried up river bed. Needless to say the fact that I was pulled off point was act of divine intervention. I walked point throughout the year's duty there. I did not receive any wounds.

During the year in Viet Nam, one night while I was praying for protection, The Lord revealed to me again He wanted me to preach. Even though I clearly heard The Lord talking to me I placed the will of The Lord in the back of my mind. Once my prayer was being answered and I was receiving protection in the battles and on point I soon forgot what I had been told about preaching. I went to Bangkok for r& r, finished my tour of duty and put preaching out of my mind.

Even though I had been raised for the greater part of my life in homes where Christianity was practiced and I had participated in church worship, my passion for Christ was a surface relationship. Even while some of my education was in a Christian school and I had read the Bible on many occasions; there was still some doubt about knowing if God was really real. I prayed because I needed to know for certain that God, Christ and His Kingdom were real. I needed proof beyond what I had been taught by others. I needed a personal revelation that left no doubt about God's existence. God answered my prayers, letting me know for certain He, Jesus, and His Kingdom were real and that He was alive. I had prayed asking God to reveal Himself to me in order that I personally would know Him as a reality. He simply talked to me quietly in my spirit until I understood His existence. He assured me I would return home from Viet Nam. Although I was afraid while walking point or in fire fights the situation never became panicky. I never became overwhelmingly homesick. There were events that happened that kept me alive that only could be classified as miracles. One incident I recall, was at that time I was pulling up the rear, or I was the last guy in the column and I had turned my back to the other Marines in the column to make sure the enemy was not coming up on us. I did not hear the Marines move out and it was some time before I discovered they had left. I did not know what direction they had gone in, in the brush out there, there were no tracks to follow. I knew I had to try and find them or I would be lost. As I made my way looking for them I caught up with them and was not captured by the enemy. To this day I doubt if any of them know I had been left.

I had volunteered when I was stationed in Marine Barracks in Norfolk, Virginia to go to Viet Nam. But going to Viet Nam was a part of God's revelation to assure me He is real. He did reveal Himself to me.

After my enlistment I resorted to living the worldly life style. I worked a while in a steel mill in Ohio. From Ohio I moved to California. I was in Pasadena and was seeking to become an actor. For relaxation on weekends I would go hiking in the foot hills around Pasadena. One Saturday when I was there God revealed without question that I was called to preach. This was about the fifth time I had been given notice that this calling was on my life. At that time I was not a student of the Scripture, but I remembered God saying to me He would prepare me so "that I would run and not get tired." I began running literally, after a few seconds I was tired. I told God He had lied to me because I was tired after running that short time. I did not understand the implications of the spiritual message that God would give endurance through the Holy Spirit to endure until the end.

Elder Richardson had told me when I was younger, he had received a revelation that some day I would preach; even though I was baptized when I was 10, I really did not take seriously what he had told me. But now in California I was certain the calling on my life to go preach was from God. I was not confused about something somebody human had told me.

Because of the revelation of the reality of God in my heart as well as in my mind, which God had given me when stationed in Viet Nam, I knew God was calling me to preach.

Even though I realized my calling was genuine I also knew I was dumb as dirt concerning what the Scriptures revealed about God and His Kingdom. And I knew I was not prepared to teach any one else. Nor was I ready to do any kind of preaching. The only thing going for me was that I knew I was called to preach. Several years earlier while I was living in Alabama a friend of mine had graduated from a Bible College in Nashville, Tn., I had attended her graduation. I decided to go back to Nashville and attend this college. The American Baptist College is the name of the college. When I arrived in Nashville, it was the last day to submit an application for that semester. I talked with the Dean of Students Dr. Lewis Powell, he told me to apply. I told him I had a G E D which I had gotten while in the Marine Corps. I also informed him that I did not have any money but was qualified to receive the GI Bill for education. He told me to go in and register.

That first semester I had not fully made the transition from the worldly life to being committed to live for Christ. I spent a lot of time watching t.v. and not studying for the classes I had enrolled in. My grades that 1st. semester were awful. James, another minister enrolled in the college and also someone from my home town of Huntsville was sent by The Lord to talk with me about my conduct. He informed me that the reason I was in college was to prepare my self to preach the Gospel and not to watch t.v. After James talked with me I became serious about my studies, the next semester my grades were a's and b's. And I kept good grades until I graduated.

I had joined Westwood Baptist University Center Church, under the Pastorate of Dr. Amos Jones, Jr. Dr. Jones gave the ministers sound training about the specifics of the duties for the Pastor and He allowed us ample opportunities to preach, conduct worship service, teach Sunday School and to carry out other functions of the church. During my studies at American Baptist College I remained a member of Westwood Church. In August of 1971 I was licensed to preach by Westwood Baptist University Center Church and in October 1973 I was ordained by Westwood Baptist University Center Church.

In 1984 I graduated from Howard University School of Divinity; with the Master's of Divinity.

All of these things and events were the early discoveries which convinced me to be converted to Christianity. After years of living with and in Christ, His power and His Spirit has revealed and assured me WHY I AM A CHRISTIAN.

Chapter 2

Faith comes by Hearing the Word

Revised Standard: Romans chapter 10: verse 17 "So faith comes from what is heard, and what is heard comes by the preaching of Christ." It is emphatically important for a seeker of Christ or any person already a disciple of Jesus to join an assembly where the Gospel of Christ is being taught as well as preached and I'll add, the Gospel is being lived out as much as possible in the lives of the people of the church.

Believe this; a disciple can only imitate the life of Jesus to the extent of the knowledge of the concepts and precepts that that individual has of Jesus' teachings and doctrines. The truth of the doctrines and principles of Christ are only found in Scriptures. To know God, His Son and His Kingdom; a disciple has to study God's word and internalize those teachings into a foundation for his or her life in which they live by. Therefore it is necessary to attend a Bible study in a church where the Pastor or Bible teacher is under the anointing of The Holy spirit. The revelation of the vision of God's Kingdom and it's benefits for the follower of Christ are taught and there is given understanding of the meaning of Scriptures. And The Holy Spirit inspires the believer to develop faith in what He/she has been taught as they heard the truth. Seek a worship that has sermon preaching and Bible teaching to help gain insight in understanding Christ's principles that you can apply them to your personal living.

Knowing more about the attributes and the roles Jesus has as the head of the church inspires the believer to want to become obligated in their duty as a disciple of Christ.

God is a ruler and he reigns over His Kingdom in His Majesty, as we are taught more of the details of His greatness and awesomeness as God we develop reverence for Him as being Absolute. We need this revelation to worship Him. This revelation has to be obtained before the disciple can successfully live as a Christian. The actual power to become a mature Christian is completely given to the disciple by the Grace of God when the disciple confess Jesus has died and arose to give them salvation. As we study the Scriptures we develop skills that explain to us what we have been given. This knowledge equips us to sustain and maintain our personal growth. The individual who is seeking to become a disciple of Christ has a function to play in his/her development as a Christian matured in the faith. We are to "work out our own salvation" by learning according to Scriptures Christ's teachings: and living day by day to grow in The Spirit and produce a life style of the fruit of the Spirit. In other words we daily must choose to walk with Christ. Discipline from the individual who wants to be Christ's disciple is the goal the person seeks. It starts with believing God is real and that God did send

His Son; Jesus to die for our sins. We believe Jesus is alive and He is able to save us as Lord. We are honest and accept responsibility for sins in our life and we ask God to forgive us for those sins through the death and resurrection of Jesus.

[1]We acknowledge that He receives us into His family as one of His children. We ask Jesus to lead us to a church where the word of God is explained and taught in order that the hearer can understand it's meaning in The Holy Spirit and then by the guidance of the Holy Spirit, the hearer can use the meaning of the word in their living.

(King James) 2 Timothy chapter 2: verse 15, "Study to show thy self approved unto God, a workman that needed not to be ashamed, rightly dividing the word of God."

(Revised standard) "Do your best to present yourself to God as one approved, a workman who has no need to be ashamed, rightly handling the word of truth." This Scripture gives us the understanding that we as disciples of Christ are obligated to invest our time in studying diligently on our own time and using our own energy to receive correct comprehension of God's word for our personal spiritual development of the truth of the Gospel of Christ.

Christian maturity helps us gain insight and knowledge about who we are as disciples of Jesus. We get revelation concerning God's gift of salvation for our personal life in

[1]   Romans chapter 10: verse 17, Revised Standard—2 Timothy chapter 2; verse 15 King James

faith. We learn about Jesus dieing for our sin, we learn about the ordeal He endured as He paid the price. We understand He is the first person God resurrected to give eternal salvation and that Jesus is the only Son God resurrected Who can give salvation. We also discover the power of Jesus and the ways His power can affect every aspect of an individuals life. Jesus' power is the source of existence in the corporate church, He empowers the victories of each Christian as we live our daily lives here on earth. Jesus gives insight into His power, the power that grants the anointing the Christian has for the ministry he/she is called into; and we are shown how this power preserves the church by our spiritual redemption which is given to us from Jesus' own righteousness. Jesus' righteousness enables us to develop the Christians obedience to God as we live day to day.

We develop spiritually when studying the word in understanding how Jesus cares for His followers. We learn that Jesus is our High Priest and as our High Priest, He prays intercessory prayers on our behalf to the Father. He reveals he is our advocate when we fall, when we sin and miss God's will for our life. He is our personal shepherd to direct our ways in this life. God teaches us that He is a God who is longsuffering and how He gives us mercy when we sin. He reveals His willingness to forgive and then work in our character to bring us into a spiritual grace where He wants us to live as we become Christ like.

God teaches us He is our provider. God teaches us he is our healer. He reveals to us He is our source of comfort and our source of joy and peace. He is our friend and He allows us to access Him regarding any issue in our life, all we need do is pray to Him concerning anything going on in our life.

We study and learn it is true, nothing is too hard for God to work out for us when we place our faith in Him and His ability to solve our crisis. We learn nothing is too hard for God to save us from. We learn God is our source both in this temporal world and in the supernatural world of His Holy Spirit. Studying enables us to birth spiritual gifts in our character as well as it enables us to acquire wisdom for the battles in this life and how to obtain power to sustain us in the warfare against the adversary.

These are some of the benefits of investing in studying diligently on our own time and in our own energy to learn the word of God that are found in the 66 books of the Bible.

Although the Old testament books teach us many things about how God revealed Himself and how He interacted in the lives of His people and others from the very beginning of creation until Jesus appeared on the scene. When a new person is coming to Jesus for salvation I suggest they start reading The New Testament Books first. The reason is simple, so they can learn who Jesus is and the work He finished when He was here on earth. And once they are familiar with the life and work of Jesus they can venture out into the books of The Old Testament. We place greater emphasis in studying the New Testament because it represents the last covenant God gave through His Son Jesus. All 66 books contain revelation of Jesus as The Messiah.

Along with the Scriptures or Bible, we need a commentary or several commentaries by different authors, and other book which expand on the Scriptures with sound or true interpretations which will enlighten the Bible. This will help us receive revelations to understand the truth of the gospel. We need to read along with reading the Bible, books of Christian authors that farther explain the epistles and will make clearer the meaning of what the Scriptures are. I suggest you talk with your Pastor or Bible teacher. To receive information concerning books and commentaries that give sound spiritual revelation.

The point is that you as a disciple of Jesus, must invest your own mind in growing as you study Jesus' Scriptures. God anointed Jesus as Christ and under His anointing, He has blessings for your life as you follow His teaching in His word in the Gospel. You can not be an effective Christian until you know His will for you from His truth as found in His word.

Along with studying His word you must invest your time in praying, (Revised Standard) Mark chapter 1, verse 24,: There fore I tell you, whatever you ask in prayer, believe that you receive it, and you will." (Revised standard) Luke chapter 6, verse 12, "In these days He went out into the hills to pray; and all night He continued in prayer to God."

Question? Why would a person who is not already a disciple of Christ or does not have a relationship with Jesus want to pray? Answer: That person needs to pray for a similar reason I would need to talk with a mathematics teacher if I wanted to solve an algebra equation. A person praying wants help with the problems they are having in their life. Prayer is the ability to have personal faith in a living God. A belief that God has a personal answer for them as He answers that prayer. An example: I stated earlier, when I was in Viet Nam, I prayed asking God – Jesus to give me the assurance that they are real and not just a fable or myth. My personal need was to know without a doubt that God was a Being Who really existed. I questioned God about His real existence and I questioned Him about attributes concerning Himself. I had heard about and I had read about Him in earlier years of life. My prayer was, if God really existed; would He make His presence alive in my life? I needed this presence from Him before I would trust and believe in Him. I needed something for a foundation for faith. (Of course, faith was the answer He gave, He filled me with Himself; only at that time I did not know that.) God answered my urgent prayer of desperation when I faced death and needed a reason to fight on, by giving me enough conviction of His existence to trust Him completely. He revealed Himself as a living Being and a God I could depend on. It was not just a guarantee for my return back home from war that caused me to pray to God. I needed a conviction that God was a living Being and that was what He gave me.

The individual praying could have one or several reasons or issues in their personal life leading them to seek knowledge for help in their life. Prayer helps that person to develop a personal faith in the living Christ. Prayer helps develop a personal conviction in the living Christ. Prayer is talking with and listening to God in Jesus' name. The needs of the heart are in an interaction with Christ with the desire that Jesus help that person in that personal prayer. After all God is your Father and he wants to help you. He wants to help you work out the concerns of your heart.

Since God created the plan of salvation through Jesus; we who follow God's plan, should ask Him to enlighten us in His word. And show us how to depend on His Holy Spirit for our salvation. Prayer and faith in God also helps us persevere while we seek His truth and after we have entered into God's redemption. (His plan for our salvation.) The truth is we as Christians survive in this life daily by turning to God and depending on Him as we pray to Jesus.

This subject is a tremendous way of life to consider. Every word of it is true. Granted it becomes personal and true for you when you have placed your faith in Jesus. Yet, as a revelation spoken by God, it is true on it's own merit as God's spoken word. It is also necessary you have accepted or you're bending toward receiving the revelation that God created the universe and that God is the creator. All that exists or has existed or will exist is God's possession by virtue of this revelation; God is the creator.

(Revised Standard) Genesis chapter 1, verse 1, "In the beginning God created the heavens and the earth.") (King James) Ephesians chapter 2, verse 10, "For we are His workmanship, created in Christ Jesus unto good works, which God hath before ordained that we should walk in them."

The scripture in the book of Genesis is a statement about the universe it self coming into existence through God, Himself speaking from His word the existence of everything that exists.

The Scripture from the book of Ephesians reveal that the power in Jesus is God's power working in the disciple of Christ because God Himself gave this power from the beginning of His creation to perfect the saints.

That revelation states the reality of God as sole owner of all, as it's creator, then that gives God the right as sole proprietor to name the plan He has put into effect to save the human race that He alone created. He as God owns and has authority over every person who has life or has lived and will live.(Revised Standard) Genesis chapter 1, verse 2, "The earth was without form and void, and darkness was upon the face of the deep; and the spirit of God was moving over the face of the waters." (Revised Standard) Genesis cha.1, verses 26-28," Then God said, "Let us make man in our image, after our likeness; and let them have dominion over the fish of the sea, and over the birds of the air, and over the cattle, and over all the earth, and over every creeping thing that creeps upon the earth." "So God created man in His own image, in the image of God, He created him, male and female He created them. "Be fruitful and multiply and fill the earth and subdue it..."

My first conviction for being a Christian is that I and all the human race was created by God and in God's image and He has sole proprietorship of my existence. If God had not created my life I would not be alive.

Genesis chapter 2 and chapter 3, reveals the sin of mankind and of which I am personally also a part of the sinfulness of disobeying God. Because I chose to disobey God's will. That being the case I along with all the human race needed to be saved from eternal condemnation. Thus the human race including myself needed God's plan of salvation.

I will ask you to read in your Bible from the book of Genesis chapters 2 and chapter 3 and discover the original fall of mankind into sin and separation from God's holiness.

The revelation is our creator God established the standard for man's moral and ethical conduct as children of God. GOD SENT JESUS AS THE EXAMPLE for us to follow. God established

His will for man's behavior and conduct. He made Jesus His method by which salvation would become man's salvation, by transferring the righteousness in the life of Jesus to man, when man proclaimed Jesus as Lord. On the other hand when man rejected Jesus as Savior man received condemnation. When man rejects the will of God, that is known as sin, as named by God. (Revised Standard) Genesis chapter 2, verses 15-17, "The Lord took the man and put him in the garden of Eden to till it and keep it. And The Lord commanded the man, saying "You may eat of every tree of the garden; but of the tree of the knowledge of good and evil you shall not eat, for in that day that you eat of it you shall die."

Here God plainly presents His will and the conduct He wants from His creation (man)

And God plainly gives the consequences that occur when man disobeys His command, His will. The consequences of disobeying God is death. The death is spiritual. Thus the need for a spiritual Savior. Also the consequence is physical death, life leaving the body of man also explaining the need for being born again to receive eternal life after we die. This is the consequence of the original sin of man.

As Creator, God already knows what His created human race would do, before God creates the human race. God made plans to rescue mankind from eternal condemnation, God is Omniscient. God has complete and through knowledge of all that will take place and all that does take place in His creation.

God's plan to rescue us, involved His Son who substituted His life for the punishment of man's sins. (New International) John chapter 3, verses 16-18, "For God so loved the world that He gave His one and only Son, "that whoever believes in Him shall not perish but have eternal life. For God did not send His Son into the world to condemn the world, but to save the world through Him." "Whoever believes in Him is not condemned, but whoever does not believe stands condemned already because he has not believed in the name of God's one and only Son." God's only plan to save mankind to have eternal salvation is in the life of His Son, Jesus.

My personal salvation as a Christian was started even back in the events of God's love and mercy occurring in the lives of Adam and Eve, along with all who trusts God to give His salvation in Christ for forgiveness in order to have eternal life. I too received grace. God's plan for all who receive salvation.

After the act of disobedience by the first family of mankind, God's initial act of mercy takes place. In this is a part of God's plan for man's salvation taking place. (Revised Standard) Genesis chapter 3, verses 22-24," Then The Lord God said, "Behold, the man has become like one of us, knowing good and evil; and now, lest he put forth his hand and take also, of the tree of life, and eat, and live for ever" therefore The Lord God sent him forth from the garden of Eden, to till the ground from which he was taken. He drove out the man; and at the east end of the garden of Eden He placed the Cherubim and a flaming sword which turned every way, to guard the way to the tree of life.

Man's gift of salvation is truly an act of mercy on God's behalf to spare man from eternal living in a state of sin.

Our revelation on behalf of God so far is:

1. God is the creator of existence and all that exists.
2. Before God created the universe He knew what actions His creation would take.
3. God already had a plan in effect to save fallen man.
4. Even though God had a plan of salvation, He gave mankind free will to decide as he desired, while God kept His truth absolute concerning the salvation process as He had commanded. He assured that His will for the destiny of man would be guaranteed.
5. God presented a phrase of mercy to spare fallen man. What He had the angles to stop in the garden of Eden was only part of His plan to save mankind. There were many other acts on God's behalf that He yet planed which would be much greater to preserve and save man.
6. Man was not judged by God, with God's justice, because man disobeyed God. Although God did not discipline fallen man for his willful disobedience to the will of God; man was spared because God's love was greater then His justice for man.
7. God knew the power that the man needed to save himself was not in man. God's plan for man's salvation demanded that God would come into the world as a man, to completely obey the will of God. This would adequately satisfy the command of God to be obeyed. God would come to earth at a later time in the form of man.

This is the primary reason that I am a Christian.

Chapter 3

Jesus Christ is God' S Plan for Salvation

In Genesis chapters 21,22, and 23 is the epic revelation of Abraham and his wife Sarah and the miraculous gift of a son, named Isaac. God tested Abraham's faith by asking Abraham to offer Isaac as a sacrifice on the alter. In obedience to God's test of his faith, Abraham decided to offer his son as a sacrifice.

(Abraham's ordeal is symbolic of the sacrifice God gave of His Son, Jesus)

Let's listen to the conversation occurring between the servants of Abraham, Isaac and Abraham and the angel of God. (Revised Standard) Genesis chapter 22: verses 5-14, "Then Abraham said to his young men" Stay here with the ass; I and the lad will go yonder and worship, and come again to you." And Abraham took the wood of the burnt offering, and laid it on Isaac his son, and took in his hand the fire and the knife. So they went both of them together. And Isaac said to his father Abraham, "My father!" And he said "Here am I, my son." He said, behold the fire and the wood; but where is the lamb for a burnt offering? Abraham said, God will provide Himself the lamb for a burnt offering, my son. "So they went both of them together.

When they came to the place of which God had told him, Abraham built an alter there, and laid the wood in order, and bound Isaac his son, and laid him on the alter upon the wood, (My comment; Isn't it interesting how obedient and willing Isaac cooperated with his father to present himself as a sacrifice?) Then Abraham put forth his hand, and took his knife to slay his son. But the angel of The Lord called to him, from heaven, and said, "Do not lay your hand on the lad or do anything to him; for now I know that you fear God, seeing you have not withheld your son, your only son, from me." And Abraham lifted up his eyes and looked, and behold, behind him was a ram, caught in a thicket by his horns; and Abraham went and took the ram, and offered it up as a burnt offering instead of his son. So Abraham called the name of that place The Lord will provide; as it is said until this day, "On the Mount of The Lord it shall be provided." And the angel of The Lord called to Abraham a second time from heaven, and said, By Myself I have sworn, says The Lord, because you have done this, and have not withheld your son, I will indeed bless you, and I will multiply your descendents as the stars of the heaven and as the sand which is on the sea shore..."

The point we take from this story in the life of Abraham and his son Isaac, God uses the events in their life to symbolically preview what God does later in the life of His only begotten Son, Jesus.

In both cases God is the One who provides the sacrifices for the offering to Him. Isaac is a photo-type of Jesus, the Son of God. Jesus said, "He laid down His life, no man could take it from Him, but of His own will He allowed Himself to be crucified.

(king James) John chapter 10: verses 17-18, "Therefore doth My Father love me, because I lay down my life, that I might take it again. No man taketh it from me, but I lay it down of myself. I have power to lay it down, and I have power to take it again. This commandment have I received of My Father." (New International) John chapter 10: verses 17-18, "The reason my father loves me is that I lay down my life, only to take it up again. No one takes it from me, but I lay it down of my own accord, I have authority to lay it down and authority to take it up again. This command I received from My Father."

The Apostle Paul illustrates the life of Jesus farther as he discusses the life of Abraham and Isaac.

In the book of Galatians, chapter 3, Paul clearly states salvation is given through faith in the life of Jesus and in what He accomplished in His life, when the disciple places faith in Jesus. (Revised Standard) Galatians chapter 3: verse 5 - 14, "Does He who supplies the Spirit to you and works miracles among you do so by works of the law, or by hearing with faith? Thus Abraham "believed God, and it was reckoned to him as righteousness." So you see that it is men of faith who are the sons of Abraham. And the Scripture, foreseeing that God would justify the Gentiles by faith, preached the Gospel beforehand to Abraham, saying, "In thee shall all nations be blessed." So then, those who are men of faith are blessed with Abraham who had faith. For all who rely on works of the law are under a curse; for it is written, "cursed be every one who does not abide by all things written in the book of the law, and do them." Now it is evident that no man is justified before God by the law; for "He through faith is righteous shall live ", but the law does not rest on faith, for "He who does them shall live by them." Christ redeemed us from the curse of the law, having become a curse for us, for it is written, "Cursed be every one who hangs on a tree", that in Christ Jesus the blessing of Abraham might come upon the Gentiles, that we might receive the promise of the spirit of faith. (Revised Standard) Galatians chapter 3: verses 23-29, "Now before faith came, we were confined under the law, kept under restraint until faith should be revealed. So that the law was our custodian until Christ came, that we might be justified by faith, But now that faith has come, we are no longer under a custodian; for in Christ Jesus you are all sons of God, through faith. For as many of you as were baptized into Christ have put on Christ. There is neither Jew nor Greek, there is neither male nor female; for you are all one in Christ Jesus. And if you are Christ's, then you are Abraham's offspring, heirs according to promise." The promise God made to Abraham, when Abraham put his faith in God's word to him, and placed Isaac before God on the alter for a sacrifice." God said to Abraham, "By Myself I have sworn says The Lord"... and I will multiply your descendants..."

Essentially, the promise Abraham received was due to faith he acted on, expecting God to fulfill His word. WHY IS THIS ESSETIAL, THAT EACH PERSON DEMONSTRATE SUCH FAITH TO BECOME A CHRISTIAN?

(New International) Romans chapter 12:verse3, "For by grace given to me I say you do not think of yourself more highly than you ought, but rather think of yourself with sober judgment, in accordance with the measure of faith God has given you." The Apostle Paul writes, disclosing to us, that, God gives to us faith, from His own riches of His kingdom. From God each saint receives, personally, the amount of faith God wants for us. We exercise our faith in God and in Christ. Christ says, faith the size of a mustard seed is sufficient; because all faith in Him or toward Him is provided by His Father, God. (Revised Standard) Matthews chapter 17; verse 20,

"He said to them, "Because of your little faith. For truly, I say to you, if you have faith as a grain of mustard seed, you will say to this mountain, "move hence to yonder place," and it will move; and nonething will be impossible to you."

Therefore, we like Abraham, can live our life pleasing God and we can complete God's will in living our life, by living and keeping Christ's commandments through the faith He gives us in His power which works in us to obey His will.

(New International) Ephesians chapter 1, verse 3-5, "Praise be to the God and Father of our Lord Jesus Christ, who has blessed us in the heavenly realms with every spiritual blessing in Christ. For He chose us in Him before the creation of the world to be holy and blameless in His sight. In love He predestined us to be adopted as his sons and (daughters) through Christ Jesus, in accordance with His pleasure and will."

The key in God's plan to save mankind all the while has been in the complete life Jesus Christ lived. God transferred Christ's righteousness into the personal life of each person who placed his or her faith in Jesus as Savior. Remembering even the ability to place our personal faith in Jesus was given by God. We have not even produced our own personal faith to believe Christ. God accessed His faith into our soul. "To the praise of His glorious grace." What God did for us by giving His faith brings praise to Him, yet we benefit by receiving His grace.

(New International) Ephesians Chapter 1, verse 7-10, "In Him we have redemption through Jesus' blood, the forgiveness of sin, in accordance with the riches of God's grace that He lavished on us with all wisdom and understanding. And He made known to us the mystery of His will according to His good pleasure, which He purposed in Christ, to be put in effect when the times will have reached their fulfillment- to bring all things in heaven and on earth together under one head, even Christ." (New International) Ephesians chapter1, verses 13-14, "And you also were included in Christ when you heard the word of truth, the gospel of your salvation, having believed, you were marked in Him with a seal, the promised Holy Spirit, Who also is a deposit guaranteeing our inheritance until the redemption of those who are God's possession-to the praise of His glory."

Again, this statement is a strong testimony of evidence to WHY I AM A CHRISTIAN, as found in (New International) Ephesians chapter 2, verses 1-10, "As for you, you were dead in your transgressions and sins, in which you used to live when you followed the ways of the world and of the ruler of the kingdom of the air, the spirit who is now at work in those who are disobedient, all of us lived among them at one time, gratifying the cravings of our sinful nature and following it's desires and thoughts. Like the rest, we were by nature objects of wrath. But because of His great love for us, God, Who is rich in mercy, made us alive with

Christ even when we were dead in transgression - IT IS BY GRACE YOU HAVE BEEN SAVED. And God raised us up with Christ and seated us with Him in the heavenly realms in Christ Jesus, in order that in the coming ages He might show the incomparable riches of His grace, expressed in His kindness to us in Christ Jesus. FOR IT IS BY GRACE YOU HAVE BEEN SAVED, THROUGH FAITH and this is not from yourselves, IT IS THE GIFT OF GOD not by works, so that no one can boast. For we are God's workmanship, created in Christ Jesus to do good works, which God prepared in advance for us to do."

Quite simply, for those who allow God to guide their thinking and their thoughts to receive Jesus as their personal Savior and Lord, becoming a Christian is an eternal gift from God. The gift happens when the believer places their faith in the person of Christ to save him or her. The event of the death by crucifixion which Christ underwent was an act of atonement for every sin of all peoples. Each person who make the choice to believe and place his or her faith in Jesus for redemption, for forgiveness and to receive salvation which comes to them; because Christ substituted Himself for their sins, receives by their faith God's gift of grace.

We as Christ's disciple do nothing in the form of the work to acquire salvation on our part. God achieves everything for the believer through the life and death and resurrection of His Son, Jesus, for the believers salvation. This is the grace we receive from God. All persons who place their faith in Jesus receives God's gift of grace. Any person who does not place their faith in Jesus for salvation does not receive the gift of grace or salvation because they have rejected God's plan for salvation. Any act of sin that was in that persons life who placed their faith in Jesus prior to believing is forgiven by God. As well as all sin the believer confesses to God after placing faith in Jesus is forgiven.

Why are we forgiven? The easiest way to state this is: It is because of God's love;

(Revised Standard) Ephesians chapter 2: verse 4, "But because of His great love for us, God, Who is rich in mercy, made us alive with Christ even when we were dead in transgressions."

Now the question is: Who does not want to receive salvation since it is a gift; and the work on our part is free? All we need do is want to receive salvation and ask God to give it to us when we place our personal faith in what Jesus has done in His life for us.

Romans chapter 10, Paul is writing to his fellow Jewish Kinsmen. His plea to them is that they let go of receiving salvation by keeping the commandments and laws that formerly had given them the promise of salvation. He wrote to them to identify for them God's new plan to receive their salvation from God by placing faith in the life, death, and resurrection of Jesus Christ. From the ladder part of the 8th. Verse through verse 11. (Revised Standard) Romans chapter 10, verse 8b; "The word is near you, on your lips and in your heart (that is, the word of faith which we preach); because, if you confess with your lips that Jesus is Lord and believe in your heart that God raised Him from the dead, you will be saved. For man believes with his heart and so is justified, and he confesses with his lips and so is saved. The Scriptures says, "No one who believes in Him will be put to shame.")

Paul says to his countrymen-The Word- Which is also The Spirit of the living Christ; is living inside the spirit in their souls, The Holy Spirit of Jesus in them gives them, their concept and precepts of the revelation and convictions of all that Christ has done. And every thing Christ has achieved for the Kingdom of God. Once they have received this revelation and conviction by The Holy Spirit from God, they now make it a personal conviction by stating in their heart through the confession by what they say to others. The weight of the confession is that the spirit of their soul has already made a committed personal confirmation of what is being stated. They are now saying that they understand that God no longer wants them to seek salvation through the process of offering sacrifices and offerings; or by keeping previous laws and commandments that were given. They now realize God has made adequate provisions for their personal salvation by offering His Son once and for all times as a sacrifice for all sins of all peoples. And when each person personally testifies that he or she believes in what has taken place through the life of Jesus; and that from that moment on, this is the method they believe in, and that they are committed to this belief for their salvation- they instantly are accepted and saved by God.

The exact and complete will of God for the person to receive faith and believe Jesus, is forever fulfilled by God's power for His or her salvation. The act of salvation is eternally finished by God.

THERE IS NO REASON TO GUESS: OR SAY PERHAPS THEY ARE SAVED: OR MAYBE THEY WILL BE SAVED, THEIR SALVATION IS GUARANTEED. For all eternity it is settled.

Their faith in Christ has finished all that God requires for their personal salvation. Period- this is God's final plan for man's salvation. Just as Paul persuaded his fellow Jewish brothers to receive God' plan of salvation in his day, the plan in today's time is the same.

Believe- God's will to save you is: By believing God allowed Jesus to substitute Himself as a sacrifice to God for your personal sins, when Jesus died on the cross. He achieved God's requirements for your personal sins. After Jesus arose from the dead He had completely satisfied God's demands. (God demanded that a human person, obey Him by doing all that He had asked, _____ Jesus fulfilled this will of God.)

Jesus personally can give to His disciples the gift of eternal salvation that God wants you to have. You can have salvation in your life now as well as when Christ returns to carry His people of His Church back to heaven with Him.

All God requires from you is to trust Him and worship Him through your faith as you personally place your faith in Jesus to save you.

Chapter 4

How God Works in the Christian Life after He Saves the Christian

It is God's promise to you, when you trust Him by faith in Jesus, to fill your life with His abundant blessings. All the issues, all the temptations, all the additions you now struggle with on a daily basis; you will find power through The Holy Spirit to cope with, and eventually The Holy Spirit will help you resolve and gain the victory in your life. And in addition, God's power of the living Christ living in you will enable you to mature your personal life as you live here on earth. The Holy Spirit will counsel and give you guidance to transform your daily existence as you receive Jesus' righteousness to live righteous as Jesus is righteous.

This transformation comes as a process; but remember Jesus has saved you already, while the process is working in your character, Jesus develops a one on one personal relationship with you. As your Savior He becomes your Shepherd. He counsels you through The Holy Spirit working in you to regenerate your thinking and your desires, or He gives you a new birth in God's Spirit. He helps your desires to change.

God does not give you Christ's righteousness and let you continue to live in the passions of sins you lived in before you placed your faith in Christ for salvation. THE GIFT OF SALVATION IS FREE. The GIFT also brings about the completion of your transformation to live for Christ. The same power of The Holy Spirit that raised Jesus from the dead after the crucifixion, has the same authority of power to destroy the hold of sin that is on the believer's life. GOD would be unloving to give you salvation and still allow you to live under the power of sin.

Yes, some people do continue to engage in activities they desired before conversion; FOR A SEASON. Perhaps their conscious is seared: perhaps they have not received correct Bible teaching etc. Still God continues to pursue that person to cause repentance in that life, that is part of the process. Some people repent immediately; for others it takes longer. The saving factor is, God never gives peace to the heart of the person in sin.

Even as God in grace gives the disciple salvation, God does a work in the disciple we call regeneration or transformation. It is simply the spiritual work of change brought on by The Holy Spirit, working in the thinking of the individual, to bring a change in the life style of the new Christian.

The Holy Spirit does a work of changing the concepts and desires from the nature of the flesh that once gave pleasure; to a new spiritual nature that brings glory to God, and edify the believer. There is not any certain length of time for this work to be completed. The Holy Spirit gives patience to the believer so that he or she does not become discouraged as The Lord fight through your weakness.

Jesus is present in you, fighting for you in the battle, and He will not quit on you. Your part is to keep faith in His ability to save you.

Yet the work of repentance does not require that the work to repent is completed by the disciple on his or her own to bring about effective change. What is required is that the disciple learns to hear the voice of Jesus speaking to him/her and obey that voice. Jesus says, to us His sheep, know His Spirit or voice and follow the instructions. (Of course, it takes a while to learn to clearly understand when you are hearing the voice of Christ.) God is in partnership with you in the work of repentance. It is the power of The Holy Spirit destroying the old ways of your life and replacing that old way with a totally new way of life for you to live. Again this is a process of time that has to take place. Yet, once the changes are evident in your life there will also occur an abundance of joy in your living. In other words I had to give up the pleasures of the world I enjoyed in the flesh in my life, before I was born again. I had to listen to The Holy Spirit and obey His counsel and instructions. I had to learn the difference between the voice of Jesus and other influences and I obeyed Jesus. And I had to learn when Satan was seeking to influence me to follow him and how to say no to Satan. And I had to learn that Satan came after me in many ways and how to avoid him in every way. To give you an example you can relate to: Florett and I married in 1993; my wife notified me, I could not smoke in the apartment we lived in. When I wanted to smoke, I would have to go outside_ rain, sleet, or snow. Imagine that in my own residence I had to go out in the rain to smoke. Well my wife was not the devil. She just did not want the drapes, or our clothes and the apartment to smell like cigarette smoke (King James) 1st. Corinthians chapter 3, verses 16,17, "Know ye not that ye are the temple of God, that the Spirit of God dwelleth in you? If any man destroy the temple of God, him shall God destroy; for the temple of God is holy. which temple ye are.) Also according to the Bible, my body as indicated in Scripture, is a temple given to me by God to be treated in a manner that will keep it healthy. Smoking causes cancer, I certainly was not treating my body in a healthy manner. The sin committed in this case was my action, smoking could bring cancer into my body and it's effects into our marriage. Sometimes during this incident Jesus spoke very clearly to me. If I continued to smoke, which would result with my body becoming contaminated with cancer; I would have to suffer the consequences. Since I knew smoking causes cancer. It would be my own actions, bringing the cancer into my body. If I continued to smoke which would result with cancer in my body, I was told by God, not to pray to Him to cure my body of cancer. Really, He told me that. He had warned me to quit. It was up to me to obey Him. He flat out told me, He would not heal me, because He had already told me to stop smoking before I was affected by cancer. The ball was now in my court; if I wanted to have peace in my home and at the same time be free from cancer, I had to decide to stop smoking. God would give me the strength to stop smoking. He would take away the taste for a smoke. But He would not come down to me to take the cigarette or cigar from my mouth. I had to want to give up the habit of smoking. God did help me stop smoking, once I prayed to Him, asking Him to help me and confessing to Him I could not stop on my own and that I needed His help. In a personal relationship with me, God removed the desire to smoke from me. It took 4 months from the time I prayed for help, for me not to desire another smoke, and I stopped completely smoking. From that day until now I have not desired to smoke. And it does not bother me to smell smoke when around other people who are smoking. I had to make some hard decisions around other smokers such as quitting several jobs, because the people insisted on smoking when I was there, even when they knew I personally did not smoke. Because I knew God's will for my life, it was not a problem to walk away from either job. Once Jesus is Lord of my life; my pleasures in life becomes the ways and activities of life which bring glory to the name of Jesus. I seek to live, participating in deeds that portray that I have surrendered to the will of Christ for my life.

Again, Paul address the subject of a Christian style of living after he/she has confessed JESUS AS LORD OF THEIR LIFE, it's found in (Revised Standard) the book of Romans chapter 7, verses 14—24, "We know that the law is spiritual; but I am carnal, sold under sin. I do not understand my own actions. For I do not do what I want, but I do the very thing I hate. Now if I do not do what I want, I agree that the law is good. So then it is no longer I that do it, but sin that dwells within me. For I know that nothing good dwells within me, that is, in my flesh. I can will what is right, but I cannot do it. For I do not do the good I want, but the evil I do not want is what I do. Now if I do what I do not want, it is no longer I that do it, but sin which dwells in me.

So I find it to be a law that when I want to do right, evil lies close at hand. For I delight in the law of God, in my inmost self, but I see in my members another law at war with the law of my mind and making me captive to the law of sin which dwells in my members. Wretched man that I am! Who will deliver me from this body of death? Thanks be to God through Jesus Christ our Lord! So then, I of myself serve the law of God with my mind, but with my flesh I serve the law of sin."

And also in (New International) Romans chapter 8, verse 1-8, "Therefore, there is now no condemnation for those who are in Christ Jesus, because through Christ Jesus the law of the spirit of life set me free from the law of sin and death. For what the law was powerless to do in that it was weakened by the sinful nature. God did by sending His own Son in the likeness of sinful man to be a sin offering. And so He condemned sin in sinful man, in order that the righteous requirements of the law might be fully met in us, who do live according to the spirit. Those who live according to the sinful nature have their minds set on what the nature desires, but those who live in accordance with the spirit have their minds set on what spirit desires. The mind of sinful man is death, but the mind controlled by the spirit is life and peace; the sinful mind is hostile to God. It does not submit to God's law, nor can it do so. Those controlled by the sinful nature cannot please God."

In this seventh chapter of Romans, Paul describes for us the classical work of the flesh's will against The Holy Spirit's will. As disciples of Christ when we read the Scriptures, we receive knowledge for us, which define for us God's will as He tells us the life style and ways He wants us to live for Him. His desire is for us to live for Him. His desire is recorded for us in His word. So we read and learn His word and because we're Jesus' disciples, it becomes our deepest desire to obey His word in our daily living. The test comes when the old life and it's nature of sin from satan from our old ways we lived, before we were born again began to surface in our lives. Satan began to push our buttons of worldly pleasures we lusted for when we belonged to him. We want the things we hungered for before we confessed Jesus as our Lord. Next we are back involved in sin we know are against the will of Christ for our lives. Yet, the spiritual man/woman yearns for the born again life of following the spirit of Jesus and not participating in old sin. We in our mind desire to live the way Christ expects us to live.

In Roman, Paul talks about the real struggle of sin in the life of a Christian. God presents His commandments which tells us what He expects from the believer, we learn and know God's will and it is our intent to obey the will of God. Yet time after time, the temptation from the influences of satan causes us to do those things we know are contrary to the will of God for our life. Therefore it becomes impossible in our own strength to fight the temptation of satan. Paul, states, I am a wretched man, because although I know what is right and sincerely I want to do the right thing, I am not always able to do God's will. Sin in me causes me to disobey God's will. Who then can save me? The answer for our dilemma is The Lord Jesus Christ. Christ's power defeats the spirit of satan in the life of the believer. As born again Christians, The Holy Spirit is transforming us by regenerating new concepts in our thinking, which changes our character and is making us new individuals. (Revised standard) 2 Corinthians chapter 3, verse 18, "And we all, with unveiled face, beholding the glory of the Lord, are being changed into His likeness from one degree of glory to another, for this comes from The Lord Who is the Spirit."

The advice we receive from Paul, is not to panic because we have not made a clean cut from sin. God is still perfecting us in His process. Satan may rear his ugly head but God is still in control. How do we know God is still in control? Jesus is the example, God gave, as the example we are to live by. The One Who has experienced each and every deed of life, that can be experienced by any human being. And because He has already wrestled with that deed, and He has already won the victory over it. He is more than able to come to your rescue and render satan's power, in you helpless and give you the victory in your personal fight against sin. Jesus rescues the believer, and brings into the disciples life, The Holy spirit's power to regenerate that person's life.

Our battle is to continue to exercise faith in Jesus, for the work He will do on our behalf. (Revised Standard) Romans chapter 8, verses 1-17, "There is therefore now no condemnation for those who are in Christ Jesus. For the law of the spirit of life in Christ Jesus has set me free from the law of sin and death. For God has done what the law, weakened by the flesh, could not do; sending His own Son in the likeness of sinful flesh and for sin, He condemned sin in the flesh, in order that the just requirement of the law might be fulfilled in us, who walk not according to the flesh but according to the Spirit. For those who live according to the flesh set their minds on the things of the flesh, but those who live according to the Spirit set their minds on the things of the Spirit. To set the mind on the flesh is death, but to set the mind on the Spirit is life and peace. For the mind that is set on the flesh is hostile to God, it does not submit to God's law, indeed it can not; and those who are in the flesh cannot please God. But you are not in the flesh, you are in the Spirit, if the Spirit of God really dwells in you, Any one who does not have the spirit of Christ does not belong to Him. But if Christ is in you, although your bodies are dead because of sin, your spirits are alive because of righteousness. If the Spirit of him who raised Jesus from the dead dwells in you, He who raised Christ Jesus from the dead will give life to your mortal bodies also through his Spirit which dwells in you.

So then, brethren. We are debtors, not to the flesh, to live according to the flesh---for if you live according to the flesh you will die, but if by the Spirit you put to death the deeds of the body you will live. For all who are led by the Spirit of God are sons of God. For you did not receive the spirit of slavery to fall back in fear, but you received he spirit of son ship. When we cry "Abba! Father!" it is the Spirit of Himself bearing witness with our spirit that we are children of God, and if children, then heirs, heirs of God, and fellow heirs with Christ, provided we suffer with Him in order that we may also be glorified with Him."

There is a verse drawn from this passage of verses that set the theme or discussion, we want to bring it out, it is verse 12: "it states that we are obligated" up until now the emphasis has been on the fact "our salvation is a gift of grace from God through faith in Jesus Christ."

Now we want to turn our attention on how we live the Christian life after we are converted. Simply put; when there are not any regulations or procedures announced for a person to live according to those standards, then that person is at liberty to live according to their personal choices.

We find in the Scriptures of the New Testament as well as The Old Testament recorded for the disciples of Christ the standard which God desires for His children to live, which will bring Him glory. These standards are God's ideal will for His children. Since God has revealed His spiritual character, and what He desires for us, when He spoke to the writers of Scripture; we are obligated to conduct our living in that manner; He has revealed in Scriptures, the goal we should focus on living toward.

This in it self makes the individual disciple" obligated. "First and foremost we are obligated to God, to live as much as possible to fulfill His standard. (With the empowering of The Holy Spirit working in us.) Because our living is a form of worship to Him, as well as an act of appreciation for all He has done for us. Our living testifies, in demonstration, who we belong to, by portraying our spiritual discernment of a life redeemed by the blood of Jesus. We are the servant of who is the master of our life.

Even when we fall from the standard of God's ideal, we find as we confess our sins and ask for forgiveness, the blood covers the fall, of our missing God's ideal. This is the reason Paul states" therefore there is no condemnation for those who are in Christ." Jesus is our sin offering, an advocate to God on our behalf. Yes as many times as we need forgiveness.

THIS IS WHY I AM A CHRISTIAN.

The next thing to discuss that's found in the 13th. verse is "but if by the Spirit you put to death the deeds of the body you will live."

Rev. Henry Harlin, Jr.

This verse brings clarity to the thought we can stop sinning with Jesus' power in The Holy spirit working in us. As disciples of Christ we are aided, we are strengthen in The Holy Spirit that raised Jesus from the dead. Sin losses it's grip on us by the Holy Spirit. The same Spirit that is God lives in us through Jesus.

Our daily living is instructed in God's agenda for us; we have help for teaching the Gospel; our life is filled with joy and nothing can keep us feeling down. We have a teacher to explain for us God's will in our life. We are not left on our own trying to find God' will for our life. God's plan and purpose for us is shown to us personally by Him. The power of Christ in us stops us from entering into temptations, whether they are physical, eating to much, getting depressed, gossiping, are what ever category that temptation appears in form of. In His power we stop seeking revenge, we get hope against discouragement, and we over come doubts. The Spirit empowers us to stop feeling sorry about the circumstances of our life and instead, gives us visions of creation, so that so that we are able to find ways that make life more positive. We cannot continue to wallow in low-self –esteem but we are made aware that as children of God we are expected to see ourselves as children of the King. He also tales away the spirit of pride and replaces that with dependence on Christ which makes us humble.

There is a long list of other gifts that God gives us that bring glory to Him and bless us. When you think of the essentials you desire in your faith for your life style, you want conditions that are honest and true. In Christianity, you have God; Who is the Creator. This same God put on a body of flesh; and came to earth to walk in the experiences

44

of man. God subjected Himself to sin. He wanted to defeat the forces of satan in order that He would liberate humanity from evil. When He placed Himself under the exposure of evil, He was victorious, and the forces of evil was conquered and it's hold on humans was destroyed. God did this by dieing in the image of Jesus. He was resurrected as Savior for mankind.

(Revised Standard) Colossians chapter 1, verses13-20. "He has delivered us from the dominion of darkness and transferred us to the kingdom of His beloved Son, in whom we have redemption, for the forgiveness of sins. He is the image of the invisible God, the first born of all creation; for in him all things were created, in heaven and on earth, visible and invisible, whether thrones or dominions or principalities or authorities__all things were created through Him and for him. He is before all things, and in him all things hold together, He is he head of the body, the church; he is the beginning, the first born from the dead, that in every thing he might be preeminent. For in him all the fullness of God was pleased to dwell, and through him to reconcile to himself all things, whether on earth or in heaven, making peace by the blood of his cross."

This Scripture speaks to the work of God in Jesus. The writer is giving praise and thanks to the Father (God); Who has made the saints able, to have access and acquire the necessary spirit and power to receive anointing to participate in the inheritance of God's righteousness.

I am leaving the book of Colossians to help enlighten it's meaning throughout the Gospel, but I will return to the book of Colossians. Jesus gave light; Jesus brought revelation; Jesus delivered the church, the believers from the kingdom of satan. Through the life of Jesus, the saints live in heaven where Christ lives with God.

We have been redeemed by the shed blood of Jesus on Calvary, where He died in atonement for sins. The Son of God; who came to earth, and was born as a child; and grew into manhood, is the exact image of the invisible God. Christ contains God's attributes.

Now this may be the first time you may have heard about God and Jesus described as being the same God. And of course you don't have any idea of the meaning involved in this description. I'll help by giving you a layman's review of the ideas in Scriptures.

1. This Scripture is not revealing that God and Jesus are two different gods. God is eternal, God is complete within Himself. He contains everything He needs to exist as God within Himself. God is Sovereign, His attributes are His and only His; alone. God maintains His own attributes. God is able to work His will by His own authority. God; Himself is YAHWEH—ELOHIM—JEHOVAH—EL-SHADDAI—ADONAI.

Yahweh is the name God identified Himself to Moses as "I Am" What ever you need; I Am able to meet your need. I am includes all God's attribute.

Elohim is The Creator God.

Jehovah is God my Father

El-Shaddi is God supplies my needs

Adonia God is my Lord, my master

2. God, is the One, Himself, Who redistributed Himself as Jesus. He configured Himself, to come to earth, in the earth realm to be born as a baby named Jesus. Jesus came into the earth realm as both, God and man. I have talked with a Physician and a University Professor who could not accept the idea that a woman could become pregnant and not have had sex with a man. God put Himself within Mary as a child. And the child was born a boy who she named Jesus.

The Scriptures reveals this event in the Gospels. (New International) St. Luke chapter 1, verses 26-38, "This is the announcement of Jesus's birth by Mary as sent to her by Angels." "In the sixth month, God sent the angel Gabriel to Nazareth, a town in Galilee, to a virgin pledged to be married to a man named Joseph, a descendent of David. The angel went to her and said, "Greeting, you who are highly favored! The Lord is with You."

Mary was greatly troubled at the words and wondered what kind of greeting this might be. But the angel said to her, "do not be afraid Mary, you have found favor with God. You will be with child and give birth to a son, and you are to name him the name Jesus, He will be great and will be called the Son of the Most High God. "The Lord God will give him the throne of his father David, and he will reign over the house of Jacob forever: His Kingdom will never end."

How will this be, "Mary asked the angel," Since I am a virgin? The angel answered, "The Holy Spirit will come upon you, and the power of The Most High will over shadow you. So the holy one to be born will be called The Son of God. Even Elizabeth your relative is going to have a child in her old age, and she who was said to be barren is in her sixth month. For nothing is impossible with God."

I am The Lord's servant, "Mary answered," May it be to me as you have said, "Then the angel left her."

Also this event is found in (New International) St. Matthews chapter 1, verses 18-25.

God sent the angel to tell Mary, she would become pregnant by The Holy Spirit of God, growing in her, to become a baby boy. Mary even mentioned to the angel, she could not understand how she could become pregnant because she was a virgin. She had never had intercourse with a man. The angel explained she would become pregnant supernaturally, by the power of God. God, Himself would grow as a baby, in her.

As we return back to the book of Colossians (New International) Colossians Chapter 1, verse 15, states "Who is the image of The Invisible God, the first born of every creature." Also (New International) Colossians chapter 1, verse 19, "For it pleased The Father that in Him should all fullness dwell." (Meaning all fullness of God was in Jesus.)

Both these verses are testimonies of the birth of Jesus by Mary and they both give description of the Godhead Being in Jesus. They verify the results of the anointing by God in Jesus, as God came Himself, to reveal His life, in a baby boy named Jesus; Who grew into manhood, to become the Savior of the world.

(New International) Colossians chapter 1, verse 14, states,: In whom we have redemption through His blood, even the forgiveness of sins." This too, verify the mission of God coming in the form of Jesus, Who is to die by crucifixion as a substitute for man, to redeem fallen man back to God's reconciliation."

(New international) Colossians chapter 1, verse 15, part b, the writer refers to Jesus as "the first born of every creature...," He is simply stating, it is by Jesus' supernatural birth, all other creatures received credibility.

It may be asked, how is that? Since Jesus was born many years after creation began? The Scriptures refers then to the writer's words in the 16th. verse. (New International) Colossians chapter 1, verse 16, "For by Him were all things created, that are in heaven, and that are in earth, visible, and invisible, whether they be thrones, or dominions, or principalities, or powers: all things were created by Him, and for Him." (New International) Colossians chapter 1, verse 17, "And He is before all things, and by Him all things exist."

Question: Who is the writer referring to in this statement, "by Him, and He is before all things?

The reference is to Jesus Himself. Jesus pre-existed with God in heaven before His birth here on earth as a human. He pre-existed as the Host of heaven in God.

Remember, we can only express and receive this knowledge in FAITH and by the guidance of The Holy Spirit in His revelation in God.

In our own carnal minds in it's thinking process, we are unable to comprehend this revelation of God. Although we seek to explain this revelation in a manner that is intelligent, the whole idea is impossible to fathom except with the aid of The Holy Spirit directing our understanding. So this supernatural knowledge and revelation concerning the existence of the life of Jesus, is received under the guidance and instruction provided in God's Spirit. We must ask God to open our minds to receive His revelation in this matter.

Again, if this is your first time being exposed to this revelation, let me suggest for your own mental spiritual well being; "You sincerely ask God to help you to understand and receive this information you are reading. "BELIEVE BY FAITH", faith meaning; God gave us His faith; or belief in Him, and His authority and power. And that He is alive. Because He lives, He is able to receive or hear your prayer request for understanding. He will give you understanding about anything you ask Him. God cares enough about you and your request to Him to give you a reply to your request. Remember, it was and is God's purpose to come to earth to save you, in order that you can have power in your life now and also to enable you to live eternally with Him, when He comes to return His Church to heaven with Him.

Speaking of the "Church" (New International) Colossians chapter 1, verse 18, "and He is the head of the body, the church: Who is the beginning, the first born from the dead that in all things He might have preeminence." (The position of being superior: having paramount rank: supreme.) He refers to Christ, the Anointed Son of God through which the spiritual existence of all believers originate. It is in the power of Jesus that the Church has it's existence. (Revised Standard) St. Matthew chapter 16, verse18," And I tell you, you are Peter, and on this rock I will build my Church, and the powers of death shall not prevail against it." Jesus is saying, He came and obeyed the complete will of God. Even to dieing. After death, which occurred under satan's power, Jesus triumph over the power of satan; when God raised Jesus back to life. In acknowledgement of His completing the will of God with His life; God established Jesus' throne forever as Lord; and established Him as head of the Church.

Because, Jesus triumphed over the power of Satan when He was resurrected; satan's power is always under the feet of Jesus. Jesus is LORD!

THIS IS THE EVIDENCE FOR THE REASON WHY I AM A CHRISTIAN.

A few of the accomplishments Jesus achieved as the head of the Church are: He intercedes or prays for repentance for sinners, and that the sinner accepts Him as Savior and Lord. He is an Advocate for those who have received Him as their Savior. He preserves or keeps the saints of the Church. He works out the will of God in the life of the saints; and He is preparing a heavenly home for the saints to live with Him forever.

Who can better save an individual from sin, into the adequate will for discipleship of Jesus; than the originator of the plan of salvation? God had His perspective for His design in mind as He declared a plan to save mankind. (Revised Standard) Colossians chapter 2, verse 9, "For in Him the whole fullness of deity dwells bodily"

When we speak of Jesus as head of the Church; we are talking about only one God. Jesus is not a separate deity from the Godhead. God emerged Himself with His own attributes into Jesus. Jesus is full of all that God consists of; All that completes God. Jesus is one hundred percent the same thing God is. Jesus is one hundred percent God.

God's love defies human understanding. How can we comprehend how God is Holy, and how He came to earth as Jesus and died for the sin of man? He literally spared us from hell by substituting Himself as an atonement in our place. That is mind blowing, yet it really happened.

(King James) 1st. John chapter 4, verse 8-10," He that loveth not knoweth not God; FOR GOD IS LOVE." In this was manifested the love of God toward us, because that God sent His only Son into the world, that we might have life through Him. Here in is love, not that we loved God, but that, He loved us, and sent His Son to be the propitiation for our sins."

Christ's anointing manifested on the behalf of the sinner is the work of propitiation, He achieved. Man, the whole race had disobeyed God's commandments. And had fallen, we were sinners.

But God allowed Jesus to stand in our place and receive punishment for our disobedience. When Jesus satisfied the requirements God demanded for the punishment of each individuals sin, He stood in as propitiation for each individual's sin.

Although the act of propitiation is for the whole human race, only the peoples who ask Christ to be the Lord of their life receives the favor of God's redemption.

YOU MUST ASK GOD THROUGH FAITH, IN THE LIFE OF JESUS, TO FOR GIVE YOU OF YOUR SINS. AND YOU MUST BELIEVE THAT JESUS DIED PERSONALLLY FOR YOUR SINS AND HIS RESURRECTION SAVES YOU. THEN YOU RECEIVE GOD'S SALVATION IN CHRIST.

Chapter 5

Master_____ Savior ___Lord of the Church___Elohim___God Creator

(King James) Genesis chapter 1, verse 1, "In the beginning God created the heavens and the earth." This expresses God's absolute Lordship. Creator, denotes a point of origin and names the Being Who is the power source. Verse 2b; "and the spirit of God was moving over the face of the waters,". When God began to create. "God said". The beginning of history; the important point of creation; is the Being of God. All that transpired was possible, because God is the person creating.

My faith in the second Person of The Trinity is established, in His Father, who is the creator of all things. THIS IS ANOTHER REASON WHY I AM A CHRISTIAN.

JEVOHAH__ THE FATHER; (Revised Standard) Genesis chapter 2, verse 7, "And The Lord God formed man of the dust of the ground, and breathed into his nostrils the breath of life; and man became a living soul." God created family. All mankind is His family. God is the Father of all mankind. There is not a race of man outside of His family. The potter's wheel of God formed our existence. God created man from the dust of the earth; God is our heavenly Father.

JEHOVAH EL- SHADDI: God my COVENANT—God my supplier. God is the founder and establisher of the contract between Himself and man. This contract is called a covenant. Which means God will do something for us, and in turn we agreed to abide by His commands. God, who is the Superior in the contract, guarantees, His created peoples, sons and daughters, that they will have their needs met. (Revised Standard) Genesis chapter 17, verses 4-8," As for me, behold my covenant is with thee, and thou shall be a father of many nations, Neither shall thou name any more be called Abram; but thou name shall be Abraham; for a father of all nations have I made thee. And I will make thee exceeding fruitful, and I will make nations of thee, and kings shall come out of thee. And I will establish my covenant between me and thee and thy seed after thee in their generations for an everlasting covenant, to be a God unto thee, and unto thy seed after thee. And I will give unto thee, the land wherein thou art a stranger, all the land of Canaan, for an everlasting possession; and I will be their God."

MASTER___SAVIOR: LORD OF THE CHURCH

(Revised Standard) Philippians chapter 2, verses 5-11, "Have this mind among yourselves, which is yours in Christ Jesus, who though He was in the form of God, did not count equality with God a thing to be grasped, but emptied Himself taking the form of a servant, being born in the likeness of men. And being found in human form He humbled Himself, and became obedient unto death, even death on a cross. Therefore God has highly exalted Him and bestowed on Him the name which is above every name, that at the name of Jesus every knee should bow, in heaven and on earth and under the earth, and every tongue confess that Jesus Christ is Lord, to the glory of God The Father."

THE LORD IS THE REASON I AM A CHRISTIAN

In the beginning of this chapter are listed a series of names for God, each name identifies a character of God's attributes which are in Jesus as Lord of the Church. There is only one God who the Christians worship, as we discuss these names of God and Jesus, I do not want to confuse you into thinking we are talking about different Gods. We are discussing the Father and the Son, both of which are the same. This is the primary reason the church can identify the source of a cult. When in the theology of an organization there is a denial of God and Jesus as the same Being; or a denial of Jesus being the Son of God; or it is said the organization worships God, but only accepts Jesus and identifies Him as a good man or a prophet, we know that that organization is a cult.

Here is only a partial list of the names of God. There are literally hundreds of names which identify the qualities of God. If you are learning about God and Jesus for the first time, it is important information to know, that Jesus gives revelation about how, He is identified as God. He explains how He comes into our lives, my life and other peoples lives. And He explains to us how He gives purpose to our lives.

Now we want to focus on Christ's Royal status. (Revised Standard) Philippians chapter 2, verse 6, clearly reveals Jesus as the "cornerstone of the Church", and as the same Spirit as God. "Who though He was in the form of God", "form" the same as God. Not an imitation of God, nor similar to God. God is Jesus in form, Jesus is God in God's form.

Verse 6b, "did not count equality with God a thing to be grasped." Jesus living in His role as a servant of God to mankind, took the position as servant more objectively as His position for the mission, He was to carry out in His work on earth. Jesus fully understood and was aware of His position of Royalty He held with God in heaven. But he was not here on earth to up hold His title, He came that He would serve mankind. Therefore He denounced His title of Royalty. He would not come as God for man to give Him glory as man gave His Father God, glory. Jesus did not want to appear in the same light as God, (Jesus did not want His light to out shine His Father's light) but He wanted to be received as a messenger for God. Of course the position that Jesus took as God's messenger or Son did not diminish His position with God; because God still accepted Jesus as He had always beheld Him in the Trinity. Jesus loved mankind and understood His mission, was to redeem fallen man back to reconciliation to a loving Father. Therefore He was not satisfied, remaining in His state of Royalty in God's form, but chose to present Himself as a vessel to God. He came as a substitute for the sins of man, and to make an atonement to pay the price required for those sins. He used His life as a servant on man's behalf to free and liberate man by paying for man's sins. He did not want to stay in heaven safely away from the ordeal of man's predicament. Instead He chose to enter into the earth realm where He would atone to God for man.

The big picture here is God came to earth, where He, God presented Himself as a man in flesh; Jesus; and died on Calvary as punishment for sin, He did not commit. God The Father was still in heaven. God The Father, did not die.

(Revised Standard) Philippians chapter 2, verse 7," But emptied Himself, taking the form of a servant, being born in the likeness of man."

Again, when we worship Jesus, we are not talking in terms of worshiping two Gods. We are talking about one God, The Godhead, Who came to live in the earth realm in a body of a man. Jesus is one hundred percent God as well as one hundred percent man. Jesus is both God and man. Yet, as Jesus He revealed qualities of the human kind, to relate to humans or mankind, on mankind's level as a human being. He identified Himself with men as a human. He, Himself subjected Himself to all the cares and confrontations that men are exposed to in their life here on earth. By exposing Himself to life in the manner in which we live, He made Himself an example of life, which we should follow in our living.

He lived life totally as we live, even to the point of obeying the will of His Father in heaven, He allowed His Father's plan of salvation to be completed, when He gave His own life on Calvary. He allowed people to kill Him as an atonement for man's sins. He took on a spirit of humbleness to God, His Father and obeyed all God commanded Him to do as a human. Jesus said, His purpose in life was to one hundred percent obey the will of God. or as He said, obeying the will of God is "His meat."

In the book of (Revised Standard) Acts, chapter 3, verses 18-26, the writer gives the prophecy of God; "But what God foretold by the mouth of all the prophets, that His Christ should suffer, He thus fulfilled. Repent, therefore, and turn again, that your sins may be blotted out, that times of refreshing may come from the presence of the Lord, and that He may send the Christ appointed for you, Jesus, Whom heaven must receive until the time for establishing all that God spoke by the mouth of His prophets of old. Moses said, "The Lord God will raise up for you a prophet from your brethren as He raised me up. You shall listen to Him in whatever He tells you. And it shall be that every soul that does not listen to that prophet shall be destroyed from the people. "And all the prophets who have spoken, from Samuel and those who came afterwards, also proclaimed those days. You are the sons of the prophets and of the covenant which God gave to your fathers, saying to Abraham, "and in your posterity shall all the families of the earth be blessed," God, having raised up His servant, sent Him to you first, to bless you in turning every one of you from your wickedness."

This is the message Peter and Paul spoke about the prophecy through out the history of Israel, that Jesus is the Messiah.

(Revised Standard) Acts chapter 13, verses 16-41, Paul is preaching in the synagogue in Antioch: "So Paul stood up, and motioning with his hand said," "Men of Israel, you that fear God, listen. The God of this people Israel chose our fathers and made the people great during their stay in the land of Egypt, and with uplifted arm He led them out of it. And for about forty years He bore with them in the wilderness. And when He had destroyed seven nations in the land of Canaan, He gave them their land as an inheritance, for about four hundred and fifty years. And after that He gave them judges until Samuel the prophet.

Then they asked for a king; a man of the tribe of Benjamin, for forty years. And when He had removed him, He raised up David to be their king; of whom He testified and said, "I have found in David the son of Jesse a man after my heart, who will do all my will." Of this man's" posterity God has brought to Israel a Savior, Jesus, as He pronounced. Before His coming John had preached a baptism of repentance to all the people of Israel. And as John was finishing his course, he said; "What do you suppose that I am? I am not He, no, but after me one is coming, the sandals of whose feet I am not worthy to untie." Brethen, sons of the family of Abraham, and those among you who fear God, to us has been sent the message of his salvation. For those who live in Jerusalem and their rulers, because they did not recognize Him nor understand the utterances of the prophets which are read every Sabbath, fulfilled these by condemning Him, though they could not charge Him with nothing deserving death, yet they asked Pilate to have Him killed. And when they had fulfilled all that was written of Him, they took Him down from the tree, and laid Him in a tomb. But God raised Him from the dead; and for many days He appeared to those who came up with Him from Galilee to Jerusalem, who are now His witnesses to the people. And we bring you the good news that what God promised to the fathers, this He fulfilled to us their children by raising Jesus, as also it is written in the second Psalm. "Thou art my son, today I have begotten thee." And for the fact that He raised Him from the dead, no more to return to corruption, He spoke this way, "I will give you the Holy and sure blessing of David," Therefore He says in another Psalm, "Thou will not let the Holy One see corruption." Let it be known to you therefore, brethen, that through this man forgiveness of sins is proclaimed to you, and by Him every one that believes is freed from every thing which you could not be freed by the law of Moses."

Chapter 6

God's Mercy

Mercy_Compassion or forbearance shown to an offender or subject: clemency: imprisonment rather than death imposed as penalty for first degree murder: a blessing that is an act of divine favor or compassion: a fortunate circumstance: relief of distress: compassion shown to the victims of misfortune, adj.

Syn. Charity, clemency, grace, lenity, mercy, implies compassion that forbears punishing even when justice demands it, charity stresses benevolence and goodwill shown in broad understanding and tolerance of others and generous forgiving or overlooking of their faults or failures; clemency implies a mild or merciful disposition in one having the power or duty of punishing; grace may combine the implications of charity and clemency. Lenity implies lack of severity in punishing.

Examples in Scripture:
(Revised Standard) Micah chapter 6, verse 8, "He has showed you, O man, what is good; and what does The Lord require of you but to do justice, and to love kindness, and

to walk humbly with your God? "Kindness being the focus word; it is the human expression of one individual in the life of another person which is an act of empathy or compassion and has a lack of harness in one's heart toward another.

(Revised Standard) 1 Timothy chapter 1, verse 13, "though I formerly blasphemed and prosecuted and insulted him, but I received mercy because I had acted ignorantly in unbelief,"

Paul, has now been converted and is now pasturing, and is giving instruction to one of his young ministers named Timothy. Paul, recalls acts he committed before he became a Christian. This particular incident he is telling Timothy about, occurs when Paul encounters Christ's Christians; Paul a devout Jewish believer, felt it was his duty to persecute Christians. As a result, many Christians were imprisoned and murdered, when Paul turned them over to the Jewish authorities.

Yet, now after Paul, himself has received Jesus as his personal Savior, and he has been commissioned by Jesus to preach the Gospel, Paul testifies God had mercy, concerning what Paul had done to Christ and Christ' Christians. God did not punish him with justice for his acts against the Christians. Paul says, he did not have the proper understanding and knowledge about who Jesus was. He was acting in the wrong belief, toward Christ and the Christians. Paul was conducting himself according to his understanding of Jewish Old Testament law. He did not understand Jesus had fulfilled the requirements of the Old Testament Law and had installed a new covenant under the grace of God. Even though, Paul had fought against Jesus, God's grace, resulted in God, giving Paul mercy.

Each individual, who realizes and accepts the death and the resurrection of Jesus as punishment, on their behalf for their sins, and that God will give them salvation; receives His mercy and His grace. God replaces punishment with mercy and grace. All that you need to do, is put your personal faith in Jesus. This is God's mercy.

It would indeed be unfortunate to have membership in any religion that did not have as a tenant of it's faith a prevision of mercy. But instead of providing mercy, to it's adherents, the people would be judged under a crude rule of merciless law, and punishment as it's doctrine, for those who were guilty of any infraction of it's order of conduct.

Life would be a miserable existence, people would be anticipating there could be at all times, someone watching their every move. While at the same time, they could realize, that day after day they lived in the fear, that unknown to them, they could be guilty of breaking some law. They would understand, when they disobeyed or broke a law the consequences would be a harsh punishment. Also the consequences would result in punishment for the offenders family and associates. Not only would the punishment come from an external power, there would be associated with the offence, a deep sense of personal guilt. And living with the result of not having the benefit of receiving mercy.

The probability of failing to obey any particular law imposed in the doctrine of that religion, would be great due to the fact of being human and not a perfect individual.

Another factor which raise the probability of failure to obey, and omit the tenants is; it would be virtually impossible to constantly remember all the rules, that if broken could result in punishment, when broken by a member of that religion.

There is just to much that happens in this fast paced world, that would keep peoples minds muddled and not clear at all times. Their minds would be engaged in other interest and concerns in the act of surviving each day. Reality will cause us to admit, somewhere, sometime, in our existence, somewhere, in some degree we have sinned, and do in fact continue to sin.

How dreadful to have to contemplate maybe having a hand cut off for stealing, or being stoned to death for committing adultery, or possibly your tongue cut out of your head for lying or because you witness some activity another person committed and you told or you did not tell about what you saw.

Maybe because, of your belief you have, your house could be blown up, or wrecked and even your family members would suffer harm or death, because you belonged to a different sect than the people around you. Even more frightening than any of these consequences, would be, that the deity who you worshipped, is not a reality, is not a living power and can not show you mercy and compassion in your failures in life. People could not appeal to the god they bowed to, to ask for mercy and pardon. What would be the hope of life?

God's mercy and love picks us up and makes us whole, when we have fallen. In the faith of Christianity, Jesus, Himself, is the sacrifice who receives the punishment so that we receive mercy and grace. Jesus offered Himself as a sacrificial Lamb as a offering to God for our sins. He took our punishment.

(Revised Standard) 1 Peter chapter 2, verse 21-25, "For to this you have been called, because Christ also suffered for you, leaving you an example, that you should follow in his steps. He committed no sin; no guile was found on his lips. When he was reviled, he did not revile in return; when he suffered, he did not threaten; but he trusted to him who judges justly. He himself bore our sins in his body on the tree, that we might die to sin and live to righteousness. By his wounds you have been healed. For you were straying like sheep, but have now returned to the Shepherd and Guardian of your souls."

Christ even showed mercy to His oppressors and executioners who crucified Him. His goal was to acquire our salvation through the suffering, He endured to acquit His disciples of their sin. He Himself never sinned. Yet, He accepted punishment, it was punishment on our behalf, so that God could give us His righteousness.

God brought us back to Himself, God reconciled us back to Him. God presented to us His mercy and grace, and allowed us to have faith for forgiveness through His love.

(New International Version) St. John chapter 15, verses 13-16, "Greater love has no one than this, that he lay down his life for his friends. You are my friends if you do what I command. I no longer call you servants, because a servant does not know his Master's business. Instead, I have called you friends, for every thing that I learned from my Father

I have made known to you. You did not choose me, but I chose you and appointed you to go and bear fruit that will last. Then the Father will give you what ever you ask in my name."

In the Gospel of John, above God reverses the position of guilt in the sinner. The person is changed from an outsider to a place of acceptance in the family of God. Faith in Jesus gives the believer a new place with God as His friend. God allows the believer to communicate with Him as Jesus does. We have to appreciate when Jesus says, "God chooses His disciples." He literally brings us into relationship with Him. No matter how dirty we are before we ask Christ to become our Lord; 0nce we ask God to forgive us, we confess our sins to Him and believe we are forgiven through Jesus, we experience for ourselves that God has chosen us for His family. The best part of all of this is that the whole process is started and is completed under the authority and power of God. When we confess to Him our sins it is because God sends His Holy Spirit into our personal mind to humble us to confess, He chooses that person. As we believe that Jesus died on the cross in our place so that we would not receive punishment, we are responding to The Holy Spirit of God. Our transformation into His family is under the power of God's Holy Spirit.

This does not imply that God picks and decides one individual over another individual. It is necessary in order to understand the action we must take, to receive salvation that The Holy spirit enables us to have the faith, to believe God will, and is doing an act of saving us. With out God allowing His power to do His work in us, we can not be saved. We can not ask for salvation by our own power, God has to open that understanding in our mind. Every person is exposed to the possibility of God giving them revelation to receive Jesus. This is God's plan of salvation for all the human race. But not all individuals will allow God to give His Spirit to them. Those who do allow His Spirit to tell them what He wants them to know, and are willing to obey Him, He chooses them to receive salvation and accepts them as His family.

The fruit of the believers life comes by the power of the Holy Spirit that is working in the life of that individual's heart. Jesus is the example that the believer is to follow as he/she lives their life. We become doers of God's word as Jesus Him Self obeyed the things that God told Him to do. Of course, we are praying asking God to give us the power to obey His will. THAT IS WHY OUR PRAYER IS IN JESUS'S NAME. God honors the name of His Son. And when our request is in the example that His Son has established, God will honor our request of prayer. Jesus tells us, we can ask any thing we want to ask and God will answer our prayer. It is the example of obeying God that Jesus has established. Can we pray to God out side of His will? Yes we can and often we do. We are human and many times we pray what our flesh wants us to ask for. It might seem right to us because we see what we are asking for as a need, and God says He will give us what we ask for in Jesus's name. I have heard people say, that at some time they had prayed to God for something or some one, really wanting what they prayed for at that time. Yet, later on they were so glad God did not answer their prayer, the way they had asked Him to. Perhaps the person they thought they wanted in their life would have been a big mistake for them. Or that particular job they were seeking would have up rooted them from their home town, they would have sold their home to move to another town, and after getting the job in a few years, the job would have faded out as the company closed down. Even in the spiritual realm people have prayed unwise prayers, something like seeking a ministry that God had not anointed them to minister in.

Therefore when we are praying, it is important that we seek the will of God, in asking for His answer. He knows the plan that He has for our lives. Now there will come times in praying when we already have a blue print of the over all plan God has for our life, and occasions occur which could disrupt His plan. And it is in His will to pray without consulting Him for what He wants. In the case of a major illness; we need to pray for healing; we already know God wants us healed; we know it is His will that His people prosper and that His people live in good health.

There was a minister, pasturing a fairly large church; from all appearances the ministry seemed genuine. From the testimonies of the members in various services, they had prayed for the success and increase of the ministries in the church. They prayed for the finances of the church. They prayed that the membership would increase, and that the members would increase in giving their tithes and their offerings to the church. They had a television ministry that broadcasted weekly. There were satellite churches in other cities from this parent church. We can be safe in saying that there were many prayers being prayed for many people involved in this ministry. What was not known through out the membership of that church, the television audience, and the public; was that drugs were sold in that ministry by the pastor. The Lord knew what was going on all the time. Although sincere prayer was being prayed by the disciples concerning the success of the ministry; God could not answer their prayers because He knew that every thing that was going on was not according to His will.

God in His mercy intervened, against the evil taking place in the midst of the congregation. The members of the congregation were stunned and hurt when the crime was disclosed. Yet, because God stopped the activity that did not glorify Him, He showed mercy to that congregation, by not allowing them to continue in that sham.

He saved them from farther embarrassment if that evil had continued in the church, both for the church, the church community, and the community at large.

Because of matters like this, and because the Kingdom of God is Holiness, He asks us to pray in the name of Jesus. Jesus always does the exact ministry or work that God tells Him to do. The result is: worship and praise goes to God.

This is how God's disciples also know that we have become children of God.

THIS IS ANOTHER REASON WHY I AM A CHRISTIAN.

We sing a song at Christmas, Santa Clauses is coming to town, he knows if we are good or bad. God is Omnipotent, Omnipresent , certainly; when God knows the number of hairs on each of our heads and He also know our thoughts before we think them. He definitely is aware of each and every activity we have been engaged in or ever will engage in, He knows if we are good or bad.

Therefore because He is an all knowing God, we need mercy. Thank God, He is merciful, long suffering and forgiving. Thank You Lord for mercy.

The book of Psalms, is full of Scripture, telling of the mercy of God. As far as that is concerned, the Bible constantly speaks of incidents, when God bestowed His mercy on man. Perhaps it is because God understands mankind plight, as is identified when David laments when he is stating this perdition in (Revised Standard) Psalm, 51, verse 1-5, "Have mercy on me, O God, according to Thy steadfast love, according to Thy abundant mercy blot out my transgressions. Wash me thoroughly from my iniquity, and cleanse me from my sin! For I know my transgressions, and my sins are ever before me. Against Thee, only, have I sinned, and done that which is evil in Thy sight, so that Thou art justified in Thy sentence and blameless in Thy judgment. Behold, I was brought forth in iniquity, and in sin did my mother conceive me.

How vivid and succinct is the picture for all mankind portrayed in these words of David. The fifth verse conveys a reality that refers to ever human born. This condition is not referring to the sexual act of intercourse in which the baby is conceived. But the reference pertains to a more profound condition of existence. It is the condition of the cosmos in which all creation exists. Verse 5, Behold, I was brought forth in iniquity; and in sin did my mother conceive me."

Here is revealed the act of man's decision to disobey God. And God's command upon all creation for the consequences resulting from the act of man in disobeying God's will. Sin was pronounced in the earth realm. So man's life was then a battle of perpetual wrestling with good and evil. This is the condition David is suggesting when he states he was "brought forth in iniquity, and in sin did my mother conceive me."

We are born to struggle in this world that is partly made up evil. Another indication of the cosmological war in which man fights is found in the Gospel, (Revised Standard) ST. Luke chapter 10, verse 18, "And He said to them," I saw Satan fall like lighting from heaven. "Christ was telling His disciples, He had given them authority to win this battle over a foe, Christ Himself had witnessed falling from heaven into the earth realm. Again Jesus gives His disciples authority to defeat unclean spirits. (Revised Standard) St. Mark chapter 6, verse 7," And He called to Him the twelve, and began to send them out two by two, and gave them authority over the unclean spirits." A very telling indication of the battle raging in the universe.

(Revised Standard) Revelation chapter 12, verses 7-12, "Now war arose in heaven, Michael and his angels fighting against the dragon, and the dragon and his angels fought, but they were defeated and there was no longer any place for them in heaven. And the great dragon was thrown down, that ancient serpent, who was called the Devil and Satan, the deceiver of the whole world-he was thrown to earth, and his angels were thrown down with him. And I heard a loud voice in heaven, saying, "Now the salvation and the power and the Kingdom of our God and the authority of His Christ have come, for the accuser of the brethren has been thrown down, who accuses them day and night before our God. And they have conquered him by the blood of The Lamb and the word of their testimony, for they loved not their lives even unto death. Rejoice then, O heaven and you that dwell there in! But woe to you, O earth and sea, for the Devil has come down to you in great wrath, because he knows his time is short."

Again this helps us interpret David's words; "iniquity and sin," when this Scripture states, "and that great dragon and his angels were defeated, the deceiver of the whole world, was thrown to earth."

The writer of the epistle of (New International) Ephesians chapter 2, verse 2, says of the devil; "in which you used to live, when you followed the ways of the world and of the ruler of the kingdom of the air, the spirit who is now at work in those who are disobedient."

All these Scriptures, as well as more scriptures in the Bible, give credence to the revelation that our world abound in evil spirits that we encounter each and every day. And these evil spirits are present to influence our way of living. So David simply stated the condition of the condition of the world he was born into; to live in, and that this world was filled with evil powers.

David never desired to deny his responsibility of acting in his own self will, of choosing to commit the sin he was involved in. He implied the cards of sin were stacked, due to the temptation of sin to allure him to submit to it's pull. (Revised Standard) Psalm 51, verse 3, "For I know my transgressions; and my sin is ever before me." David took full ownership of his disobedience to God. David confessed to God, he willfully desired to commit any act of sin he was guilty of committing. He also states he carried the guilt of his sin constantly in his conscience.

Here David performs the very thing that is needed for us to do, in order to ask God for His mercy.

We must confess to God, the sins we have committed. We also must state to God our desire to stop committing that sin; and we must stop committing that sin. (Sometimes it is an act of progress; with Jesus' Spirit taking the desire of that sin away; but the bottom line is, we stop the sin.)

Also because people are under the influence of temptation to sin, it is not a given that we must sin.

David also says to God. "God, I sinned against you." My sin may have touched other people lives, and others may have suffered from the consequences of my sins, this was secondary, to the act of sin I sinned against you. But because You are God of all, the impact of sin is against Your Holiness. I disobeyed what you commanded me not to do. I affected the personal relationship You allowed me to have with You as my heavenly Father. I rebelled against Your position as High Priest of my life. "Against You only have I sinned."

Justly, then David says to God, any and all punishment You sentence me to receive; You God are justified in rendering to me. I rightly deserve Your punishment because I have offended You in my sins.

My offense against You, have stripped me of any right of mercy; You are just in punishing me. You, God are perfect in administering, any punishment You decide to direct to my life.

But what I like about David's prayer is in Psalm 51. The first word out of David's mouth to God is: "Have mercy on me, O God."

Who of us does not need God's mercy? David's request of God implies, that David had a knowledge of the heart of God. Along with every thing else in David's world, God had given to David a special spiritual insight that, He, God was a God, Who had mercy to give to His children. David felt guilt for his sin, but he also had the gift from God to know, that God is love and that God is merciful.

It could be plausible to suggest, that the job of David shepherding sheep, contributed to his awareness of the need for mercy. For instance there may have been incidents, when a sheep or two strayed from the safety of the fold and was attacked by a bear, wolf or some other vicious animal. The sheep not being able to protect it self from the attacker, needed David to show it mercy by coming to it's rescue. David does tell us about several times when shepherding sheep and he had to do just that thing.

Yet, it would appear more credible to think about David's father, Jessie, who was a Bethlehemite, who worshipped Yahweh. And as a worshipper of the God of Israel, he had read and taught his sons, from the writings of the Septugent. And as David heard the message of the books of Moses, he was taught and he learned, among other revelations, about the mercy of God.

Some of those Scriptures could have been:

(Revised Standard) Deuteronomy chapter 4, verses 29-31, "But from there you will seek the Lord your God, and you will find him, if you search after him with all your heart and with all your soul. When you are in tribulations, and all these things come upon you in the latter days, you will return to the Lord your God, and obey his voice, for the Lord your God is a merciful God, he will not fail you or destroy you or forget the covenant with your fathers which he swore to them."

Today there are other Scriptures for our revelation: (Revised Standard) Jeremiah chapter 33, verse, 11, "There shall be heard again the voice of the mirth and the voice of gladness, the voice of the bridegroom and the voice of the bride, the voices of those who sing, as they bring thank offerings to the house of the Lord, "Give thanks to the Lord of hosts, for the Lord is good, for his steadfast love endures forever!" For I will restore the fortunes of the land as at first, says the Lord."

Another scripture is: (New International) 2 Samuel chapter 22, verse 26, "To the faithful you show your self faithful, to the blameless you show yourself blameless,"

Still another Scripture is: (New International) 2 Chronicles chapter 30, verse 9, "If you return to the Lord, then your brothers and your children will be shown compassion by their captors and will come back to this land, for the Lord your God is gracious and compassionate. He will not turn his face from you if you return to him."

The Bible reveals many promises of God's mercy. (Revised Standard) Nehemiah chapter 9, verse 31, "Nevertheless in

Thy great mercy Thou didst not make an end of them or forsake them; for Thou art a gracious and merciful God."

(Revised Standard) 2 Corinthians chapter 1, verse, "Blessed be the God and Father of our Lord Jesus Christ, The Father of mercies and God of our comfort."

(Revised Standard) Romans chapter 1, verse 1, "I appeal to you therefore, brethren, by the mercies of God, to present your bodies as a living sacrifice, holy and acceptable to God, which is your spiritual worship."

(Revised Standard) Isaiah chapter 54, verse 7, "For a brief moment I forsook you, but with great compassion I will gather you."

(Revised standard) Psalm, number 106, verse 45, "He remembered for their sake His covenant, and relented according to the abundance of his steadfast love."

Thank God for His mercy, love, and compassion. In every man, woman, and child living there was a time, there is a time and there will come a time, when God's mercy is needed and wanted. We are imperfect beings and we falter from time to time. Even in times when we know what God requires of us in our living. Thank God that He does always bring justice for our actions.

So often we hear people who have suffered an injustice in their lives, speak concerning the suspect that caused the injustice, that they want the maximum punishment for the person or persons who have wronged them; thanks to God, He does not seek the maximum justice in our lives; but He gives us mercy, even when we are guilty.

Peter reminds us of God's mercy and help to overcome the weakness in life.

(Revised Standard) 2 Peter chapter 1, verses 3-11, "His divine power has granted to us all things that pertain to life and Godliness, through the knowledge of Him who called us to His own glory and excellence, by which He has granted to us His precious and very great promises that through these you may escape from the corruption that is in the world because of passion, and become partakers of the Divine nature. For this very reason make every effort to supplement your faith with virtue, and virtue with knowledge, and knowledge with self control, and self control with steadfastness, and steadfastness with Godliness, and Godliness with brotherly affection, and brotherly affection with love. For if these things are yours and abound, they keep you from being ineffective or unfruitful in the knowledge of our Lord Jesus Christ. For who ever lacks these things is blind and shortsighted and has forgotten that he was cleansed from his old sins. Therefore, brethren, be the more zealous to confirm your call and election, for if you do this you will never fall; so there will be richly provided for you an entrance into the eternal kingdom of our Lord and Savior Jesus Christ."

The thing about mercy and it's application in the life of the believer, is, it always depends on God, Who is the one with the authority and power to make a truthful judgment pertaining to the activities in each persons life.

God has total and complete knowledge of each and every human life. It is His choice and His decision along, to give the verdict of our lives. He is always the Sovereign Being on the throne of power. The mercy we receive is always determined according to His will for us.

We have absolutely nothing to do with how He applies mercy to our lives. God is in full control of that decision.

It behooves us, to every now and then, to stop and consider the mercy He has applied to our living, and for us to fully appreciate, His mercy, and for us to show our appreciation to God, especially by the manner of life we live daily. He loves it when we show Him appreciation for the ways He has made mercy available in our lives.

When we consider, that in so many ways, our life could have taken wrong turns and we could have been destroyed; we see how dependent we are on receiving mercy from God.

Not to be boastful, we have been blessed by God's mercy in our life; but millions of other peoples just like us, for what ever reasons have not received mercy in their lives. We can not say what the reasons are they did not receive mercy in their life. Except many of the people rejected salvation through faith in Jesus alone. This would be the major reason for them to not have the mercy God wants for them in their life.

For God must remain faithful to Who He is. He can not substitute another method of salvation, for His plan of salvation. In the current affairs of the world, we witness millions of peoples every day who turn away from the gift that God presents to them, in His mercy. As a consequence of their decision to not want Jesus as their Lord and Savior, they reap the results, of the choice they make for their life. Even as much mercy as God wants to give to these individuals, He can not override the standard, He did establish as the foundation of His kingdom. And that standard is Jesus as the cornerstone of His Church.

We as God's created subjects, people who He made; we must accept His will as a guide on which our lives are constructed. Many people state that God is to loving a God to sentence punishment for sins people commit. They assume God in His love and in His mercy would allow people to live their life under the influences of their personal desires, because God is merciful.

The fortunate aspect of God's will is found in the reality, that, He has a predestined set of circumstances, in motion for the preservation and the eternal life span of people who want to live, by His mercy. He, as God, Who is Sovereign and wise, saw before He began to create the universe, all the means for life that are necessary to sustain life, both in the earth realm as well as life eternally with Him after this life.

It is not the premise with God, "of what will be will be ";: He told the early patriots of Israel; "that He set before them life and death; and it was their decision to choose which one they wanted."

Just as God gives His mercy for our lives, He obligates Himself, because of His righteousness, to withdraw from us that same mercy; and to give in it's place, His wrath when we deliberately disobey His authority. Or turn our heart from Him.

Thank God, He has a proven and guaranteed pathway of life for His people to journey, which assures our life with Him. Thank God, for His love, that He has for His children that directs our steps, that will not allow us to travel through life according to our wishes. Thank God, for His security, He gives when we listen to His voice and live the way He approves for us. Thank God, that He has a standard for living that He gives for those in His household.

Thank God, that He gives us respect, for His Holiness, to the degree that when we stray from His will for us, there is a sense of fear, of His authority over us, that over powers us and causes us to turn back to find His will for our life.

We must thank God for the love He has given us for Him, to reverence His Glory and Holiness. He has instilled in our spirit a love and a respect for Him as God in the manner, that we do not want to experience His wrath, brought on by turning away from His plans for us.

The answer to the question; would a loving God withdraw His mercy and His love? Is: When a person or people choose to disobey the will and plan God has presented to them; Yes, God will discipline that person or those individuals.

God is longsuffering or patient in bringing His punishment on People who disobey Him, but eventually, if the people refuse to repent, they will receive God's judgment.

Many Scriptures reveals this message to us about the mercy of God. (Revised Standard) The Gospel of St. Luke chapter 23, verses32-43," Two others also, who were criminals, were led away to be put to death with him. And when they came to the place which is called The Skull, there they crucified him, and the criminals, one on the right and one on the left. And Jesus said, "Father, forgive them, for they know not what they do." And they cast lots to divide his garments. And the people stood by, watching; but the rulers scoffed at him, saying, "He saved others; let him save himself, if he is the Christ of God, his Chosen One! The soldiers also mocked him, coming up and offering him vinegar, and saying, "If you are the King of the Jews, save yourself!" There was also an inscription over him, "This is the King of the Jews." One of the criminals who were hanged railed at him, saying, "Are you not the Christ? Save yourself and us!" But the other rebuked him, saying, "Do you not fear God, since you are under the same sentence of condemnation? And we indeed justly; for we are receiving the due reward for our deeds; but this man has done nothing wrong." And he said, Jesus remember me when you come in your kingly power." And he said to him, "Truly, I say to you, today you will be with me in paradise."

The example of mercy in this Scripture, is portrayed in the case of the man, who asked Jesus, to remember him when Jesus came into His Kingdom.

This man admitted, he was a man who had sinned; he said to the other man being hanged; "And we indeed justly; for we are receiving the due reward of our deeds;" he rightly accepted his punishment of being nailed on a cross, his punishment was the consequences, of the crimes he had committed. He was guilty. But Jesus looked beyond his guilt and rendered him mercy. Jesus told him "Truly; I say to you, today, you will be with me in paradise."

Jesus took away the guilt of the man's life, why? Jesus gave the man mercy, because this man recognized the holiness of Jesus! And he knew Jesus was anointed by God, and that God would establish Jesus with a Kingdom. He asked for mercy, he placed his faith in Jesus to give him mercy. The mercy he asked for was not to be based on the life's work he had committed in his life. But the mercy he asked for was to be found in the life of Jesus and on who Jesus was. The man knew Jesus had the authority to give a sentence of guilty, but he pleaded with Jesus to have mercy on him, which Jesus did.

This is essentially what God does for us, when we have faith in Jesus' death and resurrection for our personal sins. God does not see our sins, instead He sees the righteousness of Jesus, and God applies Jesus' righteousness to our lives.

Another story of mercy is found in (Revised Standard) St. Luke chapter 15, verses 11-32, "And He said, "There was a man who had two sons, and the younger of them said to the father, "Father, give me the share of property that falls to me." And he divided his living between them. Not many days later, the younger son gathered all that he had and took his journey into a far country, and there he squandered his property in loose living. And when he had spent everything, a great famine arose in that country, and he began to be in want. So he went and joined himself to one of the citizens of that country, who sent him into the fields to feed to swine. And he would gladly have fed on the pods, that the swine ate; and no one gave him anything. But when he came to himself he said," how many of my fathers hired servants have bread enough and to spare, but I perish with hunger: I will arise and go to my father, and I will say to him, "Father, I have sinned against heaven and before you; I am no longer worthy to be called your son; treat me as one of your hired servants. "and he arose and came to his father. But while he was yet at a distance, his father saw him and had compassion, and ran and embraced him and kissed him, and the son said to him, "father, I have sinned against heaven and before you; I am no longer worthy to be called your son," But the father said to his servants, "Bring quickly the best robe, and put it on him; and put a ring on his hand, and shoes on his feet; and bring the fatted calf and kill it, and let us eat and make merry; for this my son was dead, and is alive again; he was lost and is found. And they began to make merry. Now his elder son was in the field; and as he came and drew near to the house, he heard music and dancing. And he called one of the servants and asked what this meant. And he said to him, "your brother has come, and your father has killed the fatted calf, because he has received him safe and sound. But he was angry and refused to go in. His father came out and entreated him. But he answered his father, "Lo these many years I have served you, and I never disobeyed your command; yet, you never gave me a kid, that I might make merry with my friends. But when this son of yours came, who has devoured your living with harlots, you killed for him the fatted calf! And he said to him, "Son you are always with me, and all that is mine is yours. It is fitting to make merry and be glad, for this your brother was dead, and is alive; he was lost and is found."

How vividly the Scriptures reveal the love the mercy God has for His children. God's love stays the same, irregardless, of how far we stray away from His ideal conduct for us. God's love for His children does not vary. Our actions, our disobedience does not alter the love God has for us. We have to recognize God is love.

When we "come to ourselves" as the younger son in the Scriptures did, and we desire to ask God to forgive us, of whatever our sins have been, and we also ask God to help us repent, we receive mercy from Him. We need not have already repented of our sins when we ask for mercy. God wants us to realize how greatly He loves us, (even as we are now.) God wants us to desire Him in our life, and His power to guide us, in living our life. The fact is we need God's Holy Spirit to change our thoughts and our desires into the ways he wants us to live for Him.

What God asks us to do, is that we say to Him with all our being; God, I believe, You can save my life. I surrender my personal self to you; asking, you to help me, to develop a personal relationship with you, through your Son Jesus.

Father, I need Jesus to help me to organize my life. I've messed up, but I know Jesus can redeem me and salvage my life to live for you.

All I need do is return home to God, and allow Him to reveal His will for me, in regenerating my heart, and to straighten out my messed up life.

He wants to redeem us and to cover us with His covenant of mercy, through His Holy Spirit. His Holy Spirit will seal us and guarantee that the power of Jesus working in us will keep us from failing and that we will never be lost again.

In Scripture, He says, (New International) Jude verse 24, "To him who is able to keep you from falling and to present you before his glorious presence without fault and with great joy- to the only God our Savior be glory, majesty, power and authority, through Jesus Christ our Lord, before all ages, now and forevermore! Amen.)

What this Scripture says, is that Jesus guarantees to save His disciples forever, from the moment the disciple asks Jesus to become his/her Lord. In other words, from the exact moment a person comes to Christ and honestly asks, Christ to forgive him/her and to accept him/her in a personal relationship with Jesus, the personal power of Christ, which is Jesus, works in the personal life of the person, to eternally save her/him; guaranteed!

(New International) Psalm 86, verse 13, "For great is your love toward me; you have delivered me from the depths of the grave."

(New International) Psalm 94, verse 17-18, "Unless the Lord had given me help, I would soon dwelt in the silence of death. When I said, "My foot is slipping," your love, O Lord, supported me."

(New International) Psalm 103, verses 10-14, "He does not treat us as our sins deserve or repay us according to our iniquities. For as high as the heavens are above the earth, so great is his love for those who fear him; for as far as the east is from the west, so far has he removed our transgressions from us. As a father has compassion on his children, so the Lord has compassion on those who fear him; for he knows how we are formed, he remembers that we are dust."

(New International) Psalm 109 verse 26, "Help me, O Lord my God; save me in accordance with your love."

(New International) Psalm 130 verses 7-8, "O Israel, put your hope in the Lord, for with the Lord is unfailing love and with him is full redemption. He himself will redeem Israel from all their sins."

(New International) Psalm 145 verses 8-9, "The Lord is gracious and compassionate, slow to anger and rich in love, The Lord is good to all; he has compassion on all that he has made."

The message to us from these Scriptures of Psalms is that God gives to us; from his storehouse; His steadfast mercy, His compassion and His love. When we say to Him as in Psalm 109, Lord, help me. We His children receive from His storehouse, mercy.

Jeremiah reminds us in his book of (New International) Lamentations chapter 3, verses 22,23 "Because of the lord's great love we are not consumed , for his compassion never fail. They are new ever morning; great is your faithfulness."

I invite you to praise God with me in saying; this is why I am a Christian, because God gives me new mercies every morning.

Chapter 7

God is Holy, God is Glorious, God is the Perfect Father

When we decide to follow and to live our life, believing the doctrines, and trusting in the teaching, of the One Who is the authority of the Church; and Who is God of the Kingdom in which we are citizens in; we want to know with a certainty and an assurance that the God we are following is the right God. We desire to know that God is completely truthful, honest, eternal, almighty, strong and in every way able to reign in total power.

We desire a majestic God; we desire a God Who is Awesome and Sovereign in every way. We desire a God Who has real power and a God Who will operate in our lives with His power. We pray, asking God to give His wisdom to us that will enable us to discover His ways to have prosperity in our financial endeavors. We want to live wealthy lives here on earth. We want to have enough financially, so that we can help others who are in need. And we want to have more than enough for our families and our selves.

We wish to have healthy bodies and healthy minds that function with peace and without the burden of worry. Therefore we want God to heal our body, when we are sick.

We seek wisdom and knowledge to live daily, in ways that keep us from getting sick. Yet, if we do suffer illness, we want to be able to ask God to deliver us from the illness.

When our adversary attacks our life, and the battle grows beyond our effort to defend ourselves, we need a God who will defend us and defeat the enemy. We want God, who is Omniscience, to use the knowledge He has of all things in the universe; to deliver us, from things in existence that are unknown to us, yet, are known to Him.

We ask the question; can the God, we place our trust in, do the things He says He can do?

You get the picture; we expect that the God who is the head of our life, to be an all powerful God. We understand God is present everywhere at the exact same time. And we want God to have total and complete intelligence, concerning the totality of all existence. We want a God Who is the only God. And besides Him, there is no other God.

God answers the question; can He do what He says? In a conversation about Sarah, Abraham's wife, when she question God; God replied. (New International) Genesis chapter 18, verse 14, "Is anything too hard for the Lord? I will return to you at the appointed time next year and Sarah will have a son."

Our confidence in God, is instilled in us by God, who gives us faith to believe in Him.

In the Gospel (Revised Standard) of St. John, chapter 6 verses 65-69, "And He said, "This is why I told you that no one can come to me unless it is granted him by the Father."

After this many of His disciples drew back and no longer went about with him, Jesus said unto the twelve,

"Will you also go away?" Simon Peter answered him, "Lord, to whom shall we go? You have the words of eternal life; and we have believed, and have come to know, that you are the Holy One of God."

Peter spoke for all the disciples of Christ Jesus. To Whom else shall we go? God, You are the only God to go to. God, You along have all that we need for our life, now and eternally. Then Peter, says, "We have believed and we have come to know that You are the Holy One." Jesus; You are the Holy One we seek. We know, because in our journey with You, we have witnessed You using Your power, in the life of people who needed our help! We have seen the work Your Holy Spirit does for the welfare of those who need deliverance. Peter said, God You alone has the power to preserve every thing in life we need preserved. Peter said, "We have believed."

In the book of (Revised Standard) Hebrews chapter 11, verse 6, is written "And without faith it is impossible to please him. For whoever would draw near to God must believe He exists and that He rewards those who seek him."

All that we desire God to do for us in life, God does for us, God rewards us when we believe He is real and He is able to do the things we ask Him to do.

God has and is our authority, and is sovereign over every iota of existence, there is no doubt about His power. The question for us is; do we really believe God possesses Sovereign power? When we believe God, heaven is ours.

In the book of (Revised Standard) Judges in the Old Testament in chapters 6 and 7 is recorded the story where Israel' enemy, the Midinites and the Amalekites were routing Israel. These people would steal and rob Israel of the crops Israel grew to feed themselves and their live stock. When the people of Israel cried to The Lord on account of the Midianites, (Revised Standard) Judges chapter 6, verse 10, "And I said to you, "I am the Lord your God; you shall not pay reverence to the gods of the Amorites, in whose land you dwell." But you have not given heed to my voice." ...the Lord sent a prophet to the people of Israel.

When the angle of The Lord addressed the man Gideon, (Revised Standard) Judges chapter 6, verse 14, 16, "And the Lord turned to him and said, "Go in this might of yours and deliver Israel from the hand of the Midian; do not I send you?" And the Lord said to him, "But I will be with You, and you shall smite the Midianites as one man." Later on, Gideon and three hundred men with him; under the direction of God, fought for Israel; (Revised Standard) Judges chapter 7, verses 19-22," So Gideon and the three hundred men who were with him came to the outskirts of the camp at the beginning of the middle watch; and they blew the trumpets and smashed the jars that were in their hands. And the three companies blew the trumpets and broke the jars, holding in their left hands the torches, and in their right hands the trumpets to blow; and they cried, "a sword for the Lord and for Gideon!" They stood every man in his place round about the camp, and all the army ran; they cried out and fled." When they blew the three hundred trumpets, the Lord set every man's sword against his fellow and against all the army,..."

The Midinites destroyed themselves.

God fought the battle for Israel. He used Gideon to lead God's people, but God fought and won the battle. Because God is able!

Gideon, himself was a man with a low self esteem. He saw his family as weak. When the angel told Gideon about the mission God wanted him to go on, Gideon was reluctant. (Revised Standard) Judges chapter 6, verse 15, "And he said to him, "Pray, Lord, how can I deliver Israel? Behold, my clan is the weakest in Manasseh, and I am the least in my family."

God delivered Gideon from that spirit of self doubt and low self esteem. Left on Gideon's on strength, he would not have developed the courage and purpose to fight for Israel. But God, intervened, and placed courage in Gideon's heart, and redirected Gideon's attitude and thinking. God rearranged Gideon's vision with God's Spirit motivating Gideon.

This is how God works in the life of the believer. Things that seem impossible before we trusted God, become possible for us, after we and when we place our faith in Jesus. Jesus can change us and our prospective about life, once He lives inside us with His love. We have a God, who can and will create a better way for us. He can change low self esteem to great confidence and great courage. All He asks of us, is to place our faith in Him and trust Him to work on our behalf.

One of my favorite Scripture in the Old Testament is recorded in the book, 1st. Kings chapters 17-21. In these chapters are recorded how God worked through His power to reveal Himself to Israel, and other peoples. God used a man named Elijah. In this narrative of Scripture, God reveals His power and Being, as the One and only true God. The situation of the nation of Israel, was that their King had married a woman who was of the Baal religion. Baal was a pagan religion. Through this woman, Jezebel, the religion of Baal was being introduced and was being infiltrated into the nation of Israel. The people were being defiled and turning away from Yahweh to Baal worship.

God intervened and demonstrated to the people of Israel and the other nations that He is God alone.

Although a great deal of Scripture is written about Elijah, the theme of the narrative is telling how God defeated the false gods, and how God revealed the false beliefs, of the people about those false gods, Baal and Ashe'rah.

The glory and the sovereignty belongs to EL- SHADDAI.

In (Revised Standard) 1st. Kings chapter 18, verses17-19. Ahab, encounters Elijah, in a face to face meeting. "When Ahab saw Elijah, Ahab, said to him," Is it you, you troubler of Israel? And he answered, "I have not troubled Israel; but you have, and your father's house, because you have forsaken the commandments of the Lord and followed the Baals. Now therefore send and gather all Israel to me at Mount Carmel, and the four hundred and fifty prophets of Baal, and the four hundred prophets of Asherah, who eat at Jezebal's table."

Thus began the showdown where Yahweh demonstrates His Omnipotence. The irony is, Ahab, is accusing God's prophet, Elijah, of making trouble for Israel. Because Elijah is admonishing the people to quite Baal and return back to the God of Israel. Ahab had become so delusional, he could not determine who the perfect God was. He had determined his vote for Baal and Asherah and had forsaken the God EL

EL YON. Right away, Elijah corrected Ahab, and told him he was the one who had forsaken God's commandments. But then Elijah chose to challenge Ahab and his false gods to a contest of power by the real God. So Elijah says, gather all the prophets of the false gods and the people of Israel to Mount Carmel, and we'll have a contest of power to determine who will win as the real God. Elijah, says, "I will stand alone for God in this battle; as God reveals His authority and Sovereignty."

(Revised Standard) 1st. King chapter 18, verses 20-39," So Ahab sent to all the people of Israel, and gathered the prophets together at Mount Carmel. And Elijah came near to all the people and said, "How long will you go limping with two opinions? If the Lord is God follow him, but if Baal, then, follow him." And the people did not answer him a word. Then Elijah said to the people I, even I only, am left a prophet of the Lord; but Baal prophets are four hundred and fifty men. Let two bulls be given to us; and let them choose one bull for themselves, and cut it in pieces and lay wood on it, but put no fire to it, and I will prepare the other bull and lay it on the wood, but put no fire to it. And you can call on the name of your god and I will call on the name of the Lord; and the God who answers by fire, He is God." And all the people answered "It is well spoken." 'Then Elijah said to the prophets of Baal, "choose for yourselves one bull and prepare it first, for you are many; and call on the name of your god, but put no fire to it. "And they took the bull which was given them, and they prepared it, and called on the name of Baal from morning until noon, saying, O Baal, answer us. But there was no voice, and no one answered. And they limped about the alter which they had made. And at noon Elijah mocked them, saying "Cry louder, for he is a god; either he is musing, or he has gone aside, or he is on a journey, or perhaps he is a sleep and must be awaken." And they cried aloud, and cut themselves after their custom with swords and lances until the blood gushed out upon them. And as midday passed they raved on until the time of the oblation, but there was no voice; no one answered, no one heeded.

Then Elijah said to all the people, "come near to me," and the people came near to him. And he repaired the alter of the Lord that had been thrown down; Elijah took twelve stones, according to the number of the tribes of the sons of Jacob, to whom the word of the Lord came, saying "Israel shall be your name," and with the stones he built an alter in the name of the Lord. And he made a trench about the alter, as great as would contain two measures of seed. And he put the wood in order, and cut the bull in pieces and laid it on the wood. And he said, "Do it a second time;" and they did it a second time. And he said, "Do it a third time;" and they did it a third time. And the water ran round about the alter, and filled the trench also with water.

And at the time of the offering of the oblation, Elijah the prophet came near and said, "O Lord, God of Abraham, Isaac, and Israel, let it be known this day that Thou art God in Israel, and that I am Thy servant and that I have done all these things at Thy word. Answer me, O Lord, answer me, that this people may know that Thou, O Lord, art God, and that Thou has turned their hearts back. "Then the fire of the Lord fell, and consumed the burnt offering, and the wood, and the stones, and the dust, and licked up the water that was in the trench. And when all the people saw it, they fell on their faces; and they said, "The Lord, He is God: The Lord, He is God,"

The challenge Elijah brought before the people, was that they were unable to make the correct decision, about who the real God was? Elijah said, they could have a contest between God and Baal; and the one who could send fire onto the alter, would be declared the real God. Elijah said, God would provide the evidence to prove Himself, to be God. The people approved the challenge. And of course, God revealed Himself by sending fire. We today have the need of a declaration of God's reality, as Israel and the other countries in that day needed a declaration of who God was. God stands all by Himself, as the Sovereign God of the universe. But we like Elijah must be willing to testify to the truth of who God is. In a day of many alliances that people are believing in, we Christians have to stand boldly and declare there is but one God. Jesus is the answer.

Another narrative of Scripture, which reveals how God provides the resources, to sustain His children, is found in the book of Ruth. Israel was under the distress of a famine in the land. A man, Elimelech and his wife Naomi, and their sons Mahlon and Chilian, traveled to Moab to escape the famine. The sons married Moabite wives while living there. There wives names were Orpah and Ruth. Also while in Moab, Elimelech died, and later both sons of Naomi died. In the culture of that time, the source of provision for the household was the man of the house. With all three men dead, these three women were destitute. Naomi determined to return back to Israel, she felt, it would at least be best for her to die in her home land. She told her daughter in laws, that they had the option to remain in Moab and try and find husbands. Orpah decided to stay in Moab. But Ruth clung to Naomi. (Revised Standard) Ruth chapter 1, verses16-17, Ruth said; "Entreat me not to leave you or return from following you; for where you go I will go, and where you lodge I will lodge; your people shall be my people, and your God my God; where you die I will die, and there will I be buried. May the Lord do so to me and more also if even death parts me from you."

Little did Ruth know, she sealed her fate with these words.

Naomie's husband kinsman, "Boaz" allowed Ruth to pick up grain on the border of his grain field. This was how food for Naomi and Ruth to eat was gathered. One day" Boaz asked "whose maiden is this? And he was told about Ruth returning back from Moab with Naomi.(Revised Standard) Ruth chapter 2, verses 5-9," Then Boaz said to his servant who was in charge of the reapers, "Whose maiden is this?" And the servant who was in charge of the reapers answered, "It is the Moabite maiden, who came back with Naomi from the country of Moab. She said, "Pray, let me glean and gather among the sheaves after the reapers." So she came, and she continued from early morning until now, without resting for a moment." Then Boaz said to Ruth, "Now, listen, my daughter, do not go to glean in another field or leave this one, but keep close to my maidens. Let your eyes be upon the field which they are reaping, and go after them. Have I not charged the young men not to molest you? And when you are thirsty, go to the vessels and drink what the young men have drawn."

(Revised Standard) Ruth chapter 2, verse 11-12, "But Boaz answered her," All that you have done for your mother in law since the death of your husband has been fully told me, and how you left your father and mother and your native land and came to a people that you did not know before. The Lord recompense you for what you have done, and a full reward be given you by the Lord, the God of Israel, under whose wings you have come to take refuge!"

According to tradition in Israel; the nearest kin in the family had first option to Ruth, also any land that Elimelech had left Naomi could be bought by the next of kin.

(Revised Standard) Ruth 3, verses 12-13, "And now it is true that I am a near kinsman, yet there is a kinsman nearer than I. Remain this night, and in the morning, if he will do the part of the next of kin for you, well; let him do it; but if he is not willing to do the part of the next of kin for you, then, as the Lord lives, I will do the part of the next of kin for you. Lie down until the morning."

The next day Boaz approached the next of kin concerning the matter of Ruth's mother in laws land, and if he wanted to purchase it.

(Revised Standard) Ruth chapter 4, verses 1, 3-6, "And Boaz went up to the gate and sat down there; and behold the next of kin, of whom Boaz had spoken, came by. So, Boaz said, "Turn aside friend, sit down here," and he turned aside and sat down."

Verses 3-6; "Then he said to the next of kin, Naomi, who has come back from the country of Moab, is selling the parcel of land which belonged to our kinsman Elimelech. So I thought I would tell you of it, and say, buy it in the presence of the elders of my people, if you will redeem it, redeem it, but if you will not tell me, that I may know, for there is no one besides you to redeem it, and I will come after you." And he said' I will redeem it." Then Boaz said, the day you buy the field from the hand of Naomi, you are buying Ruth the Moabitess, the widow of the dead, in order to restore the name of the dead to his inheritance. Then the next of kin said, "I can not redeem it for my self, lest I impair my own inheritance," take my right of redemption yourself, for I cannot redeem it."

(Revised Standard) Ruth chapter 4, verse 13, 14a "So Boaz took Ruth and she became his wife; and he went in to her, and the Lord gave her conception, and she bore a son. Then the women said to Naomi, "Blessed be the Lord, who has not left you this day without next of kin;"

God saw the need of Naomi and Ruth and made arrangements for their welfare even before they left Israel for Moab. God protected them in their journey returning back to Israel. God directed both Ruth's and Boaz's steps until they had completed His plan. God set the right people in place to be used as His vessels. Of course, Naomi, Ruth, and Boaz and their household benefited from the results guided by God in their lives, but the major performance for the destiny of all the people involved, was under the control of the Spirit of God. The revelation that is revealed in their lives as well as for our lives is that, God provide resources for His people, in their time of crises. We have a God Who has the ability to work supernatural wonders, in our life, when we look to Him for His support. Christians do not need to play the lottery, expecting and hoping for help in our life. We have a sure source for our life's expectations to come into our life; and it's all in the power of our living God.

The book of Esther tells us how God protected Israel, in His glorious might and His miraculous authority. The book of Esther tells how the Jewish people were saved from annihilation by the Persians and the Medes people; and in particular an Agagite man by the name of Haman. The book of Esther has ten chapters, I invite you to, in your leisure to read the entire book. I'm writing from partial Scripture to tell, the events which demonstrated, God delivering His people from destruction. We know that when an individual approached the throne of a King, the King had to extend his scepter or the individual would be rejected; if the scepter was extended the person was accepted by the King. In the first chapter of Esther, there was an act that was even more astonishing, (Revised Standard) Esther chapter 1, verse 3, "King Ahasu-erus gave a banquet, for all his princes and servants, the army chiefs of Persia and Media and the nobles and governors of the province before him." (Revised Standard) Esther chapter 1, verse 10a,11, 12, "On the seventh day, when the heart of the King was merry with wine, he commanded ...," verse 11, "to bring Queen Vashti before the King with her royal crown, in order to show the peoples and the princes her beauty; for she was fair to behold. But Queen Vashti refused to come at the King's command conveyed by the eunuchs. At this the King was enraged, and his anger burned within him." (Revised Standard) Esther chapter 1, verse14_20, "the men next to him,..., who saw the King's face, and sat first in the kingdom_:" According to the law, what is to be done to Queen Vashti, because she has not performed the command of King Ahasu_erus conveyed by the eunuchs? Then Memucan said in presence of the King and the princes, "not only to the King has Queen Vashti done wrong, but also to all the princes and all the people who are in all the provinces of King Ahasu_erus. For this deed of the Queen will be made known to all women, causing them to look with contempt upon their husbands, since they will say, King Ahasu_erus commanded Queen Vashti to be brought before him, and she did not come. This very day the ladies of Persia and Medis who have heard of the Queen's behavior will be telling it to all the King's princes, and there will be contempt and wrath in plenty. If it pleases the King, let a royal order go forth from him, and let it be written among the laws of the Persians and the Medes so that it may not be altered, that Vashti is to come no more before King Ahasu_erus; and let the King give her royal position to another who is better than she."

(Revised Standard) Esther chapter 2, verses5,7-10, "Now there was a Jew in Susa the capitol whose name was Mordecai, the son of Jair, son of Shimei, son of Kish, a Benjaminite," verse 7, "He had brought up Hadassah, that is, Esther, the daughter of his uncle, for she had neither father nor mother; the maiden was beautiful and lovely; and when her father and her mother died, Mordecai adopted her as his own daughter. So when the King's order and his edict were proclaimed, and when many maidens were gathered in Susa the capitol in custody of Hegai, Esther also was taken into the King's palace and put in custody of Hegai who had charge of the women. And the maiden pleased him and won his favor; and he quickly provided her with her ointments and her potion of food, and with seven chosen maids from the King's palace, and advanced her and her maids to the best place in the harem. Esther had not made known her people or kindred, for Mordecai had charged her not to make it known." (Revised Standard) Esther chapter 2, verse16,17, 19-23, "And when Esther was taken to King Ahasu-erus into his royal palace in the tenth month,..." verse 17, "the king loved Esther more than all the women, and she found grace and favor in his sight more than all the virgins, so that he set the royal crown on her head and made her queen instead of Vashi." Verses 19-23, "When the virgins were gathered together the second time. Mordecai was sitting at the King's gate. Now Esther had not made known her kindred or kindred or her people, as Mordecai had charged her; for Esther obeyed Mordecai just as when she was brought up by him. And in those days, as Mordecai was sitting at the King's gate, Bigthan and Teresh, two of the King's eunuchs, who guarded the threshold, became angry and sought to lay hands on King Ahasu-erus. And this came to the knowledge of Mordecai, and he told it to Queen Esther, and Esther told the King in the name of Mordecai. When the affair was investigatd and found to be so, the men were both hanged on the gallows. And it was recorded in the book of the chronicles in the presence of the King."

The authority, the presence, and the power of God; Who is a living God, is on display in this Scripture. Even before Israel and the people of Israel are exiled into captivity; God has planned the events that will occur in the country they are exiled into.

Vesthi would be dethroned, and a new queen would be placed on the throne. God had Esther there at this particular time, to use her when the occasion arose to serve Him, to save His people from destruction. She became a chosen vessel to bring glory to God.

The difficulty in the lives of the Jews was worsening, an enemy was gathering his forces and people with the goal of destroying the Jewish people. But before this could happen, The Lord put His plan into action.

(Revised Standard) Esther chapter 3, verses1-6; 8-11; "After these things King Ahasu-erus promoted Haman the son of Hammedatha the Agagite, and advanced him and set his seat above all the princes who were with him. And all the King's servants who were at the King's gate bowed down and did obeisance to Haman; for the King had so commanded concerning him. But Mordecai did not bow down or do obeisance. Then the King's servants who were at the King's gate said to Mordecai, "Why do you transgress the King's command?" And when they spoke to him day after day he would not listen to them, they told Haman, in order to see whether Mordecai's words would avail; for he had told them that he was a Jew. And when Haman saw that Mordecai did not bow down or do obeisance to him, Haman was filled with fury. But he disdained to lay hands on Mordecai alone. So, as they had made known to him the people of Mordecai, Haman sought to destroy all the Jews, the people of Mordecai, throughout the whole kingdom of Ahasu-erus." Verses 8-11," Then Haman said to King Ahasu_erus, "There is a certain people scattered abroad and dispersed among the people in all the provinces of your kingdom; their laws are different from those of every people, and they do not keep the King's laws, so that it is not for the King's profit to tolerate them. If it please the King, let it be decreed that they be destroyed, and I will pay ten thousand talents of silver into the hands of those who have charge of the King's business, that they may be put into the King's treasuries." So the King took his signet ring from his hand and gave it to Haman the Agagite, the son of Hammedatha the enemy of the Jews. And the King said to Haman, "The money is given to you, the people also, to do with them as it seems good to you."

You had better believe, the moment you decide to live your life obeying the Lord, attacks from the enemy will try to disrupt your obedience to Jesus; even though; Jesus is working on your behalf to lift you above the disruption; God moves according to His will in the situation, some times it seems He is not present. We have to learn to have faith in Jesus and His will for our life.

(Revised Standard) Esther chapter 4, verses, 1-3, "When Mordecai learned all that had been done, Mordecai rent his clothes and put on sackcloth and ashes, and went out into the midst of the city, wailing with a loud and bitter cry; and he went up to the entrance of the King's gate, for no one might enter the King's gate clothed with sackcloth. And in every province, wherever the King's command and his decree came, there was great mourning among the Jews, with fasting and weeping and lamenting, and most of them lay in sackcloth and ashes."

When God has set the course for His disciple, none thing can detour it!

(Revised Standard) Esther chapter 4, verses, 5-17, "Then Esther called for Hathach, one of the King's eunuchs, who had been appointed to attend her, and ordered him to go to Mordecai to learn what this was and why it was. Hathach went out to Mordecai in the open square of the city in front of the King's gate, and Mordecai told him all that had happened to him, and the exact sum of money that Haman had promised to pay the King's treasuries for the destruction of the Jews. Mordecai also gave him a copy of the written decree issued in Susa for their destruction, that he might show it to Esther and explain it to her and charge her to go to the King to make supplication to him and entreat him for her people. And Hathach went and told Esther what Mordecai had said. Then Esther spoke to Hathach and gave him a message for Mordecai saying, "all the Kings servants and the people of the King's provinces know that if any man or woman goes to the King inside the inner court without being called, there is but one law; all alike are to be put to death, except the one to whom the King holds out the golden scepter that he may live. And I have not been called to come in to the King these thirty days." And they told Mordecai what Esther had said. Then Mordecai told them to return answer to Esther, "Think not that in the King's palace you will escape any more than all the other Jews. For if you keep silence at such a time as this, relief and deliverance will rise for the Jews from another quarter, but you and your father's house will perish. And who knows whether you have come to the kingdom for such a time as this?" Then Esther told them to reply to Mordecai, "Go gather all the Jews to be found in Susa, and hold a fast on my behalf, and neither eat nor drink for three days, night nor day. I and my maids will also fast as you do. Then I will go to the King, though it is against the law; and if I perish, I perish." Mordecai then went away and did everything as Esther had ordered him."

(Notice Mordecai's statement of faith, in God's providential protection of the Jews.

"for if you keep silent at such a time as this, relief and deliverance will rise for the Jews from another quarter..." God's word would never fail and God had promised He would be Israel's God and Israel would be His people, Mordecai knew God is able!)

(Revised Standard) Esther chapter 5, verses 2-4, "And when the King saw Queen Esther standing in the court, she found favor in his sight and he held out to Esther the golden scepter that was in his hand. Then Esther approached and touched the top of the scepter. And the King said to her, "What is it, Queen Esther? What is your request? It shall be given you, even to the half of my kingdom." And Esther said, "If it please the King, let the King and Haman come this day to a dinner that I have prepared for the King."

(Again, God is arranging the details of Haman's destruction which Haman speaks from his own mouth.)

(Revised Standard) Esther chapter 5, verses 10-14 "Nevertheless Haman restrained himself, and went home;

and he sent and fetched his friends and his wife Zeresh. And Haman recounted to them the splendor of his riches, the number of his sons, all the promotions with which the King had honored him, and how he had advanced him above the princes and the servants of the King. And Haman added, "Even Queen Esther let no one come with the King to the banquet she prepared but myself. And tomorrow also I am invited by her together with the king. Yet all this does me no good, so long as I see Mordecai the Jew sitting at the king's gate." Then his wife Zeresh and all his friends said to him, "Let a gallows fifty cubits high be made, and in the morning tell the king to have Mordecai hanged upon it; then go merrily with the king to the dinner." This counsel pleased Haman, and he had the gallows made."

(Revised Standard) Esther chapter 6, verses 1-11, "On that night the King could not seep; and he gave orders to bring the books of memorable deeds, the chronicles, and they were read before the king. And it was found written how Mordecai had told about Bigthana and Teresh, two of the king's eunuchs, who guarded the threshold, and who had sought to lay hands upon King Ahasu-erus. And the king said, "what honor or dignity has been bestowed on Mordecai for this? The king's servants who attended him said, "nothing has been done for him." And the king said, "who is in the court?" Now Haman had just entered the outer court of the king's palace to speak to the king about having Mordecai hanged on the gallows that he had prepared for him. So the king's servant told him, "Haman is there, standing in the court." And the king said, "Let him come in." So Haman came in, and the king said to him, "what shall be done to the man whom the king delights to honor?" And Haman said to himself, "Whom would the king delight to honor more than me?" And Haman said to the king, "for the man whom the king delights to honor, let robes be brought, which the king has worn, and the horse which the king has ridden, and on whose head a royal crown is set; and let the robes and the horse be handed over to one of the king's most noble princes; let him array the man whom the king delights to honor, and let him conduct the man on horse back through the open square of the city, proclaiming before him: Thus shall it be done to the man whom the king delights to honor." Then the king said to Haman, "Make haste, take the robes and the horse, as you have said, and do so to Mordecai the Jew who sits at the king's gate. Leave out nothing that you have mentioned." So Haman took the robes and the horse, and he arrayed Mordecai and made him ride through the open square of the city, proclaiming, "Thus shall it be done to the man whom the king delights to honor."

(Again Haman, not knowing what he was saying, spoke from his mouth a blessing on the life of Mordecai.)

(Revised Standard) Esther chapter 7, verse 1-10, "So the king and Haman went in to feast with Queen Esther. And on the second day, as they were drinking wine, the King again said to Esther, "What is your petition, Queen Esther? It shall be granted you. And what is your request? Even to the half of my kingdom, it shall be fulfilled." Then Queen Esther answered, "If I have found favor in your sight, O King, and if it please the king, let life be given me at my petition, and my people at my request. For we are sold, I and my people, to be destroyed, to be slain, and to be annihilated. If we had been sold merely as slaves, men and women, I would have held my peace: for our affliction is not to be compared with the loss to the king." Then King Ahasu-erus said to Queen Esther, "Who is he, and where is he, that would presume to do this?" And Esther said, "A foe and enemy! This wicked Haman!" Then Haman was in terror before the king and the Queen. And the king rose from the feast in wrath and went into the palace garden; but Haman stayed to beg his life from Queen Esther, for he saw that evil was determined against him by the king. And the king returned from the palace garden to the place where they were drinking wine, as Haman was falling on the couch where Esther was; and the king said, "will he even assault the queen in my presence, in my own house?" As the words left the mouth of the king, they covered Haman's face. Then said Harbona, one of the eunuchs in attendance on the king, "moreover, the gallows which Haman has prepared for Mordecai, whose word saved the king, is standing in Haman's house, fifty cubits high." And the king said, "Hang him on that." So they hanged Haman on the gallows which he had prepared for Mordecai. Then the anger of the king abated."

God flipped the scene on Haman, all that Haman had planned to do to the Jews suddenly came down on his head. Yes, God will use, any body, every day people as He did Esther to accomplish His purpose! When we are willing to become His instrument. Esther made her self available to be used for God, when she made the statement; "if I perish, I perish". She sold out to God, holding none thing back. It was not just offering her life as a sacrifice, that Esther was concerned with; but she was relying on the greatness of God Who she worshipped. Esther's faith in her decision to go before the king rested on God' promise to always be God of His people Israel.

(Revised Standard) Esther chapter 8, verse 9-11," The king's secretaries were summoned at the time, in the third month of Silvan, on the twenty-third day; and an edict was written to all that Mordecai commanded concerning the Jews to the satraps and the governors and the princes of the province from India to Ethiopia, a hundred and twenty seven provinces, to every province in its script and to every people in its own language, and also to the Jews in their script and their language. The writing was in the name of King Ahasu_erus and sealed with the king's ring, and letters were sent by mounted couriers riding on swift horses that were used in the king's service, bred from the royal stud. By these the king allowed the Jews who were in every city to gather and defend their lives, to destroy, to slay, and to annihilate any armed force of any people or province that might attack them, with their children and women, and to plunder their goods,"

There are numerous accounts in Scripture, telling us how God works in His providential power. We as people need, God's help and salvation, in every aspect and area of our life. When we seek Him, He comes to us in every way we need Him. Although God has warehouses of blessings

He has reserved to give us; it is only when we asks Him to bless us, these blessings become ours. Do not fear to ask God to bless your life, your family, your church. When we ask in faith, our heavenly Father will answer our prayer according to His riches in heaven.

We who are Christians, worship Jesus, of Whom the Scriptures says: in the book of (Revised Standard) Colossians chapter 1, verses 13-20. "He has delivered us from the dominion of darkness and transferred us to the kingdom of his beloved son, in whom we have redemption, the forgiveness of sins. He is the image of the invisible God, the first-born of all creation; in heaven and on earth, visible and invisible, whether thrones or dominions or principalities or authorities__ all things were created through him and for him. He is before all things, and in him all things hold together. He is the head of the body, the church; he is the beginning, the first born from the dead, that in every thing he might be preeminent For in him all the fullness of God was pleased to dwell, and through him to reconcile to himself all things, whether on earth or in heaven, making peace by the blood of his cross."

God is Supreme, above all things; as He explains Himself, as He and Jesus are: when He tells us Jesus is the image of His attributes. God, expresses Himself to us, in a language that we understand as humans. From this language, we learn of the greatness of God; yet, in this Scripture of Colossians; God speaks to us about His Son Jesus. God tells us, Jesus, as Himself, "is above all things, for He created all things, on earth and in heaven, visible and invisible. From the book of

Genesis in the Old testament, we read that God created the universe and the heaven; in Colossians, God said; He, Jesus created all things; indicating Jesus is the same as God, His father." All things were through Him and for Him"; again God says, the power that God operates with, is the same power that Jesus operates with. "He is before all things"; we know God, only is before all things; by God saying; Jesus is before all things, God is saying; as Himself, Jesus is as He is, God is. And, "He is the head of the body, the church"; Jesus is the Founder and Executive of all believers or disciples, who are Christians; by this work Jesus did in His life. Jesus, alone, is the sacrificial Lamb; Who died on Calvary, for the sins of all peoples. Jesus, alone was resurrected by God; thereby securing victory, over Satan and his forces, for the salvation of mankind. The life of Jesus, and His works alone are the Corner stone on which the Church is built.

God, is God alone. God is our all and all; and when we place our faith in Who He is, He develops with us a personal relationship. The relationship He develops in us is; God is out Father and we are His children. Jesus as our Savior, is the mediator, or go between God and us. Every thing that belongs to God becomes ours also. We inherit through Christ, every thing that belongs to Christ. All that God has given Christ is ours also. Our faith in Christ gives us full inheritance with Him from God. From A to Z, every thing we need to live a full and successful life is ours. By faith in Christ alone. This is the testimony of God to us. Because He could not find anyone else He could trust completely, He placed the fulfillment of His word in Himself; for all things needed, and completed His plan His self. Even the faith needed by us to trust Christ in faith, comes from God. God deals to us the correct measure of faith, He gives to us our faith!

The Old Testament writers spoke of God and His power in these Scriptures:

(Revised Standard) Psalm 86, verses 8-10, "There is none like Thee among the gods, O Lord, nor are there any works like thine. All the nations thou hast made shall come and bow down before thee, O Lord, and shall gloify thy name. For thou art great and doest wondrous things, thou alone art God."

In the New Testament, Paul the apostle, preaching on one occasion in Athens, spoke of God Who is the maker of heavens and earth. (Revised Standard) Acts chapter 17, verses 23-32," For as I passed along, and observed the objects of your worship, I found also an alter with this inscription, "to an unknown god." What therefore you worship as unknown, this I proclaim to you. The God who made the world and everything in it, being Lord of heaven and earth, does not live in shrines made by man, nor is he served by human hands, as though he needed any thing, since he himself gives to all men life and breath and everything. And he made from one every nation of men to live on all the face of the earth, having determined allotted periods and the boundaries of their habitation, that they should seek God, in the hope that they might feel after him and find him. Yet he is not far from each one of us, for "in him we live and move and have our being." As even some of your poets have said, "for we indeed are his offspring." Being then God's offspring, we ought not to think that the Deity is like gold, or silver, or stone, a representation by the art and imagination of man. The times of ignorance God overlooked, but now he commands all men everywhere to repent, because he has fixed a day on which he will judge the world in righteousness by a man whom he has appointed, and of this he has given assurance to all men by raising him from the dead." Now when they heard of the resurrection of the dead, some mocked, but others said, "We will hear you again about this."

The man Paul spoke concerning this when he said, He who was resurrected from the dead is Jesus.

To close out this chapter, and the discussion of the Almighty God, are listed several scriptures depicting God's final plan, of victory over all His enemies. These Scriptures tell of the crucifixion and the resurrection of Jesus; which gave us then and still continues to give salvation, to mankind. When we place our faith in believing, Jesus died for our sins, and by His death and His resurrection from the dead; God gives us salvation in His grace.

(Revised Standard) St. Matthews chapter 26, verses 26-29, "Now as they were eating, Jesus took bread and blessed it, and gave it to the disciples and said, "Take eat; This is my body." And he took a cup, and when he had given thanks he gave it to them," Saying, "Drink of it, all of you; for this is my blood of the covenant which is poured out for many for the forgiveness of sins. I tell you, I shall not drink again of this fruit of the vine until that day, when I drink it new with you in my father's kingdom."

In this verse Jesus is having His "last supper" with His disciples before He is betrayed; falsely accused; falsely judged; and crucified. Here He is prophesying about the events which will take place, including events after His resurrection and His returning to heaven, where again He will have supper with His disciples and He will drink of the cup with them.

The events of God's providence, working for the salvation of mankind are recorded in the 27th chapter of St. Matthew. Again I ask that you read these verses in your leisure time as you read the entire chapter. Here are details of the sequence of events which led up to the crucifixion of Jesus.

(Revised Standard) St. Matthew chapter 27, verses 35-37, 50: "And when hey had crucified him, they divided his garments among them by casting lots; then they sat down and kept watch over him there." And over his head they put the charges against him, which read, "This is Jesus the King of the Jews." Verse 50; "And Jesus cried again with a loud voice and yielded up his spirit."

(Revised Standard) St. Matthew chapter 27, verses 57-60, "When it was evening, there came a rich man from Arimathea, named Joseph, who also was a disciple of Jesus. He went to Pilate and asked for the body of Jesus. Then Pilate ordered it to be given to him. And Joseph took the body, and wrapped it in a clean linen shroud, and laid it in his own new tomb, which he had hewn in the rock; and he rolled a great stone to the door of the tomb, and departed.

(Revised Standard) St. Matthew chapter 28, verses 1-10, "Now after the Sabbath, toward the dawn of the first day of the week, Mary Magdalene and the other Mary went to see the sepulcher. And behold, there was a great earthquake; for an angel of the Lord descended from heaven and came and rolled back the stone, and sat upon it. His appearance was like lighting, and his raiment white as snow. And for fear of him the guards trembled and became like dead men. But the angel said to the women, "do not be afraid; for I know that you seek Jesus who was crucified. He is not here; for He is risen, as He said. Come, see the place where He lay. Then go quickly and tell his disciples that He is risen from the dead, and behold, He is going before you to Galilee; there you will see him. Lo, I have told you." So they departed quickly from the tomb with fear and great joy!" And ran to tell his disciples. And behold Jesus met them and said, "Hail!" And they came up and took hold of his feet and worshipped him. Then Jesus said to them, "do not be afraid, go and tell my brethren to go to Galilee, and there they will see me."

At the conclusion of this event, all opposing forces and all adversaries of God had been defeated. Satan and all spirits of his, were placed under the feet of Jesus!

God showed Himself Supreme!

THIS IS WHY I AM A CHRISTIAN.

My faith is in Jesus, I believe He died to forgive all my sins, and He arose to give me salvation; He substituted His life as a substitute for my life.

I believe God accepted, the punishment Jesus took; for me and for every human who will ever live.

THIS IS GOD'S PLAN OF SALVATION FOR EVERY HUMAN BEING.

THIS IS WHY I AM A CHRISTIAN.

Let me invite you to receive Jesus as your Savior; by saying to Him, you believe He died and arose for you. Tell The Lord, you want to become His disciple, that you want to become a Christian.

Order Form _____

Rev. Henry Harlin, Jr.
4049 Scotwood Dr.
Nashville, Tn. 37211
Tel. (615) 331-0144
henryharlinjr@att.net

Date: _____

ORDERED BY:(PLEASE PRINT) _____

NAME: _____
ADDRESS: _____
CITY: _____ STATE: _____ ZIP CODE: _____
TELEPHONE: _____

Sales Person: _____

Buyer's Signature: _____

Quality: _____   ISBN: <u>978-1-4908-4668-2</u>
Title: <u>Why I Am a Christian</u>
Description: <u>5x8 Perfect Bound Soft Cover</u>
Unit Donation: <u>$11.95</u>
Total: _____

_____ Copies @ $11.95

Shipping: $3.00 first Book, $1.00 each add. Book _____

TOTAL _____

C O D By special arrangements:

Prepaid and Credit Card:

___Master Card   ___ Visa   Exp. Date_____

Signature_____

Revised Standard: Mark chapter 11, verse 24; Revised Standard: Luke chapter 6, verse12; Revised Standard; Genesis cha. 1, verse1; King James Ephesians cha.2 verse 10
Revised Standard Genesis cha. 1, verse 2; Genesis cha.1, verse26-28
Revised Standard Genesis chapter 2, verses 15-17
New International John chapter 3, verses 16-18
Revised Standard Genesis chapter 3, verses 22-24
Revised Standard Genesis chapter 22: verses 5-14

King James John chapter 10: verses 17-18
Revised Standard Galatians chapter 3: verses 5-14
Revised Standard Galatians chapter 3: verses 23-29

New International Romans chapter 12: verse 3
Revised Standard Matthew chapter 17: verse 20

New International Ephesians chapter 1, verses 3-5
New International chapter 1, verses 7-10
New International Chapter 1, verses 13-14
Revised Standard Ephesians chapter 2, verse
King James 1st. Corinthians chapter 3, verses 16,17
Revised Standard Romans chapter 7, verses 14-24
Revised Standard Roman chapter 8, verses 1-8
Revised Standard 2nd. Corinthians chapter 3, verse 18
Revised Standard Romans chapter 8, verses 1-17
Revised Standard Colossians chapter 1, verses 13-20
New International St. Luke chapter 1, verses 26-38
New International St. Matthews chapter 1, verses 18-25

New International Colossians chapter 1, verse 15
New International Colossians chapter 1, verse 19
New International Colossians chapter 1, verses 14, and verse 15b
New International Colossians chapter 1, verse 16 and verse 17
New International Colossians chapter 1, verse 18
Revised Standard St. Matthew chapter 16, verse 18
Revised standard Colossians chapter 2, verse 9

King James 1st. John chapter 4, verses 8-10

King James Genesis chapter 1, verse 1

Revised Standard Genesis chapter 2, verse 7

Revised Standard Genesis chapter 17, verses 4-8

Revised Standard Philippians chapter 2, verses 5-11

Revised Standard Philippians chapter 2, verse

Revised Standard Acts chapter 3, verses 18-26

Revised Standard Acts chapter13, verses 16-41

Revised Standard Micah chapter 6, verse 8

Revised standard 1 Timothy chapter 1, verse 13

Revised Standard 1 Peter chapter 2, verse 21-25

Revised Standard Psalms, 51, verses 1-5

Revised standard St. Luke chapter 10, verse 18

Revised standard St. Mark chapter 6, verse 7

Revised standard Revelation chapter 12, verses 7-12

New International Ephesians chapter 2, verse 2

Revised Standard Psalm 51, verse 3

Revised standard Deuteronomy chapter 4, verses 29-41

Revised Standard Jeremiah chapter 33, verse 11

New International 2 Samuel chapter 22, verse 26

New International 2 Chronicles chapter 30, verse 9

Revised Standard Nehemiah chapter 9, verse 31

Revised Standard 2 Corinthians chapter 1, verse 3

Revised Standard Romans chapter 12, verse 1

Revised Standard Isaiah chapter 54, verse 7

Revised standard Psalm, number 106, verse 45

Revised standard 2 Peter chapter 1, verses 3-11

Revised Standard St. Luke chapter 23, verses 32-43

Revised Standard St. Luke chapter 15, verses 11-32

New International Jude verse 24

New International Psalm 86, verse 13

New International Psalm 94, verses 17-18

New International Psalm 103 verses 10-14

New International Psalm 109 verse 26

New International Psalm 130 verses 7-8

New International Psalm 145 verses 8-9

New International Lamentations chapter 3, verses 22,23
New International Genesis 18, verse 14
Revised Standard St. John chapter 6, verses 65-69
Revised Standard Judges chapter 6, verse10
Revised Standard Judges chapter 6, verses 14,16
Revised standard Judges chapter 7, Verses 19-22
Revised Standard Judges chapter 6 verse 15

Revised Standard chapter 18 verses 17-19
Revised Standard 1st. Kings chapter 18, verses 20-39
Revised Standard Ruth chapter 1, verses 16,17
Revised Standard Ruth chapter 2, verses 5-9
Revised Standard Ruth chapter 2, verses 11,12
Revised standard Ruth chapter 3, verses 12,13
Revised Standard Ruth chapter 4, verses 1, 3-6
Revised Standard Ruth chapter 4, verses 13,14a
Revised Standard Esther chapter 1 verse 3
Revised Standard Esther chapter 1, verses 10a, 11, 12
Revised Standard Esther chapter 1, verse 14-20
Revised Standard Esther Chapter 2, verses 5, 7-10
Revised Standard Esther chapter 2, verses 16,17, 19-23
Revised Standard Esther chapter 3, verses1- 6, 8-11
Revised Standard Esther chapter 4, verses 1-3
Revised Standard Esther chapter 4, verses 5-17
Revised Standard Esther chapter 5, verses 2-4
Revised Standard Esther chapter 5, verses10- 14
Revised Standard Esther chapter 6, verses 1-11
Revised Standard Esther chapter 7, verses 1-10
Revised Standard Esther chapter 8 verses 9-11
Revised Standard Colossians chapter 1 verses 13-20
Revised Standard Psalm 86, verses8-10
Revised Standard Acts chapter 17, verses 23-32
Revised Standard St. Matthew chapter 26, verses 26-29
Revised Standard St. Matthew chapter 27, verses34,35,50
Revised Standard St. Matthew chapter 27, verse 57-60
Revised Standard St. Matthew chapter 28, verses 1-10